REPAIRING
Pottery & Porcelain

A Practical Guide

Second edition

LESLEY ACTON & PAUL McAULEY

The Lyons Press

Guilford, Connecticut

An imprint of The Globe Pequot Press

First published in Great Britain 1996 by Herbert Press

This edition 2003 by
A & C Black Publishers Limited
Alderman House, 37 Soho Square, London W1D 3QZ
www.acblack.com

ISBN:0-7136-6241-7

Published simultaneously in the USA by The Lyons Press

ISBN: 1-59228-024-2

A CIP catalogue record for this book is available from the
British Library and the US Library of Congress

Front cover illustration: Staffordshire figurine
Frontispiece: Worcester figure of a Dutch boy

Designed by Jo Tapper

Cover design Dorothy Moir

All photographs by Zul Mukhida

Printed and bound in Malaysia by Times Offset (M) Sdn. Bhd

Contents

Acknowledgements

The authors would like to thank all those who made this book possible, directly or indirectly! To everybody at A&C black and to Zul at Chapel Studios – we never knew a photo-shoot was such hard work, we learnt a lot! Credit has to go to Martina Catinelli, for her brilliant work, and the loan of her hands; also to Peter 'Tex Sing' Pollard and Stacey we appreciate all your help.

From Paul:

I would like to thank all my colleagues along the way, especially those in Lincoln; and to Josephine for her encouragement and support.

From Lesley:

Thank you to my brother Paul, for his unswerving help and support in all of my endeavors; also to my parents who enabled me to eat – by doing the shopping while I was otherwise engaged writing.

To James and Lauren, both of whom have grown somewhat since the first addition of this book, your mother is immensely proud of you and everything you have achieved thus far. I know this is only the beginning for both of you.

This last year has brought many changes, but one of the best is my Professor! Thank you for being my rock.

Introduction

Many people assume that once broken, a ceramic object has come to the end of its useful life. While this *may* be true of purely functional wares, with a methodical approach and the help of modern materials, decorative ceramics can be repaired. Ceramic restoration has a long history and a great number of materials and techniques have been employed over the years. There is evidence from as far back as 7000BC of holes being 'drilled' into pots and the use of fibre 'ropes' to bind together fragments.

In the past much faking took place and there was a tendency to over-restore. Today there is much more emphasis on honest and sympathetic repair work. It is important however, to appreciate historical repairs as they can tell us much about the ethical approach and the fashions of the times in which they were carried out. These repaired artifacts are often the only evidence of historical repair methods and materials. Documentation was not usually considered an integral part of the repair process, and therefore knowledge of the history of ceramic restoration, at least in written form, is scant.

Removal of historic restoration should be carefully considered. Where it is not actively contributing to the

Below: front and back of soft paste porcelain tea plate showing rivetted repair

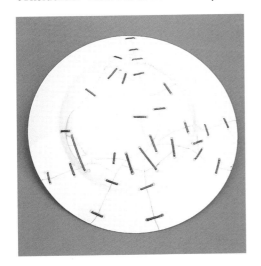

deterioration of the object, or obscuring important detail, then it may be in the best interest of the object to leave it well alone. Current conservation practice today is usually to seek a less proactive role than that which had been originally thought acceptable.

This book aims to guide the student, the amateur and the professional restorer through each and every stage of restoration, tackling the simple, the difficult, and the seemingly impossible jobs, and to provide practical information on every aspect of the ceramic repair process.

Ceramic repair poses many problems – from removing a previous poor or discoloured restoration, to the challenge of correctly dismantling, rebonding and aligning shards, and the filling and colour matching of missing areas. All of these are potentially difficult tasks, but by following the guidelines and advice of this book, making trial runs and testing materials before applying them to the object, satisfactory results can be obtained.

Weights and measures are given in metric terms, with US and imperial versions in brackets (e.g. US pints and gallons).

A full glossary of materials is included at the end of this book. This gives all relevant US alternative product names, as well as giving a brief description of the product and indicating its hazardous properties.

Conservation and restoration

There is much made today of the terms 'conservation' and 'restoration' and of the distinction between them. What exactly do these terms mean and how do they apply to ceramic repair? *The Oxford English Dictionary* gives the following definitions:

> *Conserve*: to keep from harm or damage, to preserve especially for later use
> *Restore*: to bring back or attempt to bring back to the original state by rebuilding, repairing, repainting etc.

Thus the conservator's purpose is to stabilise an object and to prevent further deterioration, and any sensitive restoration should embrace this conservation element, as well as involving other aspects such as replacing missing parts and retouching. It must be remembered that the very nature of the material we are dealing with is inherently fragile, and that there are few pieces with any history which are not damaged in some way. The term 'repair' is used in this book to encompass both conservation and restoration.

Anyone carrying out a ceramic repair treads a fine line between doing so much work to a piece that it makes it look as though it was made yesterday, or so little that he or she fails to perform the basic duty of stabilising and conserving. Whatever the balance, there are a few basic rules to follow:

- Not to inflict any further damage by misuse of tools or materials or by careless handling
- To make sure each stage is reversible, i.e. by using materials that can be removed completely and with minimum intervention, even in the long term
- To preserve the integrity of the object by carrying out honest repairs without the intention to deceive
- All applied materials must be compatible with the fabric of the object

Many old restorations are 'bodged' attempts at repair – frequently too much adhesive has been applied causing misalignment, unsuitable materials have been used in gap fills and, most commonly, over-painting has occurred in an attempt to disguise a poor repair. It is challenging to effect a complete colour match, but in conservation terms this may not always be the best solution. A well-executed fill in a shade close to the body colour, which is then left as it is, is preferable to a poor attempt at colour matching, or, worse, over-painting on top of the original material. Although in some cases the owner may demand an invisible repair, the more honest approach is preferable and avoids any criticism of over-restoration.

One question which occupies many people is whether the restoration of an object detracts from its value. While it is true that over-restoration can certainly reduce the value of an object, there is no doubt that sympathetic work can at the very least make it more aesthetically pleasing.

There are several professional conservation associations that offer guidance to students and practising professionals. These associations organise conferences and seminars, and many of them also publish professional journals. They are invaluable in educating, updating, and furthering the development of professional skills. A full list of these organisations is given in the appendix section on p.111. In the United Kingdom, the Institute for Conservation has now instituted an accreditation programme. Conservator-restorers are required to demonstrate competence and professionalism in their work, as well as adhering to the profession's code of practice. Once accredited, members are further required to undergo an annual review to demonstrate ongoing professional development.

Notes on the care of ceramics

- Repaired ceramics should no longer be considered suitable for any further use except display
- To clean a repaired ceramic use a small damp sponge, and if necessary a weak detergent solution – *do not immerse in water.* If the object is very dusty, rinse in lukewarm water and pat dry with a clean tea towel or kitchen roll. If you are dusting particularly vulnerable objects, remove them from the display area, place on a secure cushioned surface and dust with a large, soft, squirrel-haired artist brush
- Repaired ceramics should neither be displayed in direct sunlight nor kept in a dark cupboard
- Do not lift any repaired ceramic by its handle; always lift with both hands, using one hand to support the base
- Keep vulnerable objects in safe places, i.e. in display cabinets. These in turn should be placed in an environment that is not subjected to constant changes in temperature or humidity
- If you are storing objects, then use acid free tissue to wrap them. If you need to transport objects ensure that they are correctly wrapped and securely stowed during transportation

1. Tools and materials

There are certain items that are fundamental to the restorer's needs. It is wise to buy materials only as you need them, thus avoiding both the expense of an initial outlay and also the risk of buying expensive pieces of equipment and materials which you may find you are unable to use.

However, there are certain tools and materials that you will need to stock up on before commencing any repairs. Table 1 (overleaf) lists the basic, intermediate and advanced kits needed to carry out competent repairs safely and efficiently. By acquiring tools and materials according to these categories you may gradually build up a comprehensive range.

A selection of tools and materials

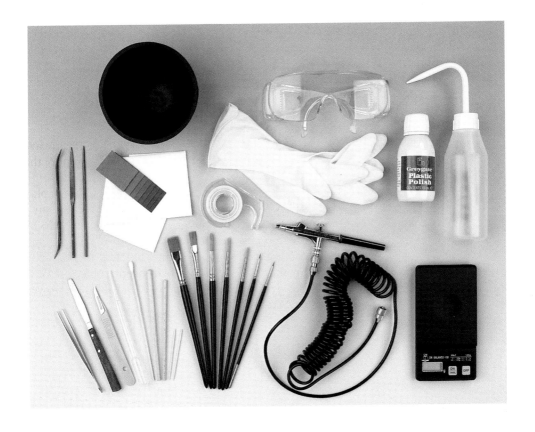

Table 1. Repair kits

TOOLS	MATERIALS
Most basic kit	
A range of artists' brushes	Acetone
Cocktail or wooden sticks	Artists' acrylic paints and glazes
Cotton wool and tissues	Biological washing powder
Disposable gloves	Cellulose nitrate adhesive
Fine abrasive or garnet paper	Cling film (plastic wrap)
Forceps/tweezers	Non-ionic detergent liquid
Magnifying glass	Paraloid B-72
Safety spectacles	Plaster e.g. Polyfilla
Scissors	Plasticine
Scotch magic tape	
Small craft knife	
Small metal or plastic spatula	
Small pliers	
White ceramic tiles	
Intermediate kit	
All the above plus:	
Acid-free tissue	A range of solvents
Bubble wrap	Artists' powder pigments
Disposable pipettes	Bronze powders
Good quality artists' brushes	Bulking agents, e.g. talc & fumed silica
Rubber mixing bowl	Dental wax sheets
Set of small files or rifflers	Epoxy adhesive/casting resin
Solvent dispenser bottle	Epoxy putty (Milliput)
Swann Morton scalpel blades,	Hydrogen peroxide & ammonia
e.g. 10, 10a, 11, 13,15	Instant adhesive (superglue)
Swann Morton scalpel handles	Jenolite rust remover
No. 3 or 4	Micromesh polishing cloths
	Silicone moulding materials & release agent
Advanced kit	
Airbrush with compressed air supply	Araldite colours
Airbrush cleaning fluid	Gilder's kit & gilding materials
Masking films and tapes	Poulticing materials
Mini digital scale	
Photographic scale	
Room thermometer	
Stereo microscope	
Vernier calliper	

Support methods

Various items can be used to support objects while the adhesive is curing (drying) or while a mould is setting. These can range from adhesive tape (preferably the gentle 'magic tape' variety) and re-usable modelling material such as plasticine, to rubber bands and small specialist clamps. For delicate objects that need to be placed on their side, a cork ring or soft bean bag (or even a bag of salt) can be used, or the ceramic can be placed in a tray filled with polystyrene (styrofoam) balls.

Health and safety

Many jobs carry health and safety risks. The main risks that arise from this type of work are from contact with epoxy resins and solvents, and inhalation of dust or paint particles.

A solvent is a liquid used to dissolve other substances. Frequently-used solvents in this book are acetone, dichloromethane (Nitromors), white spirit (mineral spirits) and industrial methylated spirit (IMS/denatured alcohol). Solvents can enter the body by inhalation or by skin contact. They may cause effects such as irritation of eyes/lungs/skin, headaches and nausea.

- Solvent inhalation can be avoided by adequate ventilation and/or the use of extraction equipment
- Contact dermatitis can be prevented by using latex or nitrile gloves and/or a barrier cream
- Dust/paint inhalation can be prevented by wearing a proprietary face mask
- Eye protection should be worn when using sharp tools such as scalpels, or when using chemicals or spraying paint
- Use scalpels with care; when putting on and removing blades from handles use a pair of pliers or blade removers

There is now a legal requirement for manufacturers to supply material safety data sheets or appropriate labelling for all hazardous materials. These sheets will give all the information needed, for example, about the composition of the product, hazard identification,

Figure 1.

Hazard symbols

Toxic substances which present a serious risk of acute or chronic poisoning by inhalation, ingestion or skin absorbtion.

Harmful substances which present moderate risk to health by inhalation, ingestion or skin absorption.

Flammable extremely flammable liquids have a flash point of less than 0° and a boiling point less than or equal to 35°C.

Highly flammable liquids include:
1. those which may become hot and finally catch fire in contact with air at ambient temperature without application of energy.
2. those which may readily catch fire after brief contact with a source of ignition and which continue to burn or to be consumed after removal of the source of ignition.
3. those which are gaseous and flammable in air at normal pressure.
4. those in contact with water or damp air which evolve highly flammable gases in dangerous quantities.
5. liquids which have a flash point below 21°C.

Highly flammable liquids are those having a flash point equal to or greater than 21°C and less than or equal to 55°C.

Oxidising substances which give rise to highly endothermic reactions in contact with other substances particularly flammable substances.

Corrosive substances which destroy living tissue.

Irritant substances which are non-corrosive but are liable to cause inflammation through immediate prolonged or repeated contact with the skin or mucous membranes.

usage, first aid measures, and disposal methods. Ask your supplier to provide these and always read the instructions to find out about possible dangers (see Glossary of materials on p. 111). In the UK, COSHH guidelines (control of substances hazardous to health) are published by HMSO (see opposite). In the USA, information can be obtained from the National Institute of Occupational Safety and Health, Washington DC.

The information contained in a material safety data sheet should be used to prepare a risk assessment for any potentially hazardous materials. A risk assessment will evaluate and identify hazards and where possible, control, reduce or remove them. This may be in the workplace, i.e. buildings, ventilation, noise, etc. or with materials used in the workplace. All risk assessments should be recorded.

Additionally, the studio should be equipped with a first aid kit and an eye wash kit. It is also advisable to wear some form of protective clothing such as a laboratory coat or coverall, gloves, eye protection as well as face masks suitable for the appropriate hazard.

Storage
Health and safety regulations in most countries require appropriate storage for any hazardous material and especially solvents. All potentially hazardous material should be stored in a sheet steel fireproof cupboard that is finished in safety yellow and carries appropriate labelling on the outside. Any substances decanted from original containers must be put into suitable receptacles and also carry appropriate labelling.

Disposal
Do not pour out or mix up any more of the chemicals than you are likely to need for the job in hand. This is not only wasteful, but increases the problems of disposal. Proper disposal techniques will vary according to the chemical and the locale, and you should always refer to the material safety data sheet for the correct disposal method.

A place to work in
Ideally, you need a well-lit north-facing room with good ventilation. The work environment should not be in a room that is subjected to extreme changes in

temperature and humidity. Even such a stable group of artifacts such as ceramics can be affected by constant changes in temperature and humidity, especially some porous bodied wares, which may be particularly vulnerable to a fluctuating environment.

You will also require a sink for washing the objects in, workbenches, shelves and appropriate storage cupboards. A small trolley on wheels is also a very useful addition to hold hand tools and materials that are used frequently. Obviously the size of the room is dependent on how much work one intends to do, and therefore how much storage space one needs. Some form of air extraction equipment is needed both for the removal of fumes from any solvent-based products that may be used and for when using an airbrush to spray paint.

Figure 2 (opposite) shows a simple DIY air extraction unit which has been erected on the workbench. Timber supports are used as a frame, on which perspex sheets have been overlaid and fixed into position. A small air extraction unit is placed approximately midway inside the unit on an outside wall. The front panel should be positioned to protect the face from any paint or solvent spray, but allowing access to the object so that it may be worked on. A small turntable is a useful addition for repositioning an object while retouching. There are a number of companies today that make small portable extraction booths, and these are ideal where space is at a premium. However, remember any such unit must be maintained on a regular basis in order to provide optimum efficiency.

Lighting

Good lighting is essential. It is important in that it enables you to examine the object properly, and also for checking further stages, for example to allow you, once the object has been filled, to see the blemishes in the filling. Appropriate lighting is especially vital when retouching an area, because if this is not done under the correct lighting conditions then the match of the paint may well be less than perfect, which will cause the retouched area to show. Ideal lighting conditions are those in which there is a north-facing light and the restorer is sitting sideways on to this light. This will rarely be available and consequently artificial aids such as a daylight light bulb in an anglepoise lamp, or a day-

Figure 2.
Conservation studio with air extraction unit

light tube in an overhead fluorescent-type fitting can provide a good source of correct lighting. These bulbs and tubes are available from most good lighting retailers, hobby shops or conservation suppliers.

Metamerism

When a mixture of colours (particularly blue or a mixture containing blue) is viewed, the same colours may look quite different in varying lighting conditions. This variation is known as 'metamerism' and is an important factor to take into consideration when retouching or making coloured fills. If at all possible, work should be arranged so that colour matching takes place during that part of the day when natural daylight is at its optimum. This is particularly relevant during winter, when bright natural daylight may only be available for a limited period each day.

Thought must also be given to the display of restored objects, objects should be retouched or filled (where coloured fills are appropriate) under the same lighting conditions in which they are to be displayed.

2. Examination and identification

Examining the object

The first stage of ceramic repair is to examine the object in order to identify the ceramic body and to decide how to approach the repair process. If an object has been previously repaired it may have adhesive or filling material covering large areas, it may be rivetted, its joints may be badly aligned or it may be completely overpainted. For all these reasons it is difficult to make a treatment plan until the object has been cleaned and you are better able to identify its needs. Sometimes you may simply be presented with a bag of pieces, in which case these should be laid out in jigsaw fashion and the examination carried out as described below.

Any examination of the object should be carried out in excellent lighting conditions and possibly with the use of a handheld magnifying glass. A small binocular microscope can be another valuable aid not only in the initial examination, but also in any subsequent stages of treatment such as removal of any dirt or contaminating matter, or when aligning edges during rebonding.

You are looking, particularly at this stage, for cracks that may not easily be seen, for chips, any missing parts, and any damage to the piece which may render it unstable or which may involve extra care. Sometimes the piece is very dirty or it is covered in glue or has been previously restored in such a way that it is difficult to see what has to be done. In this case, you should follow the cleaning instructions given in the next chapter and clean the piece appropriately before returning to the examination. This should be done anyway on any piece that needs anything more than a simple clean.

Treatment record
When beginning any repair it is important to start a treatment record on which all relevant information can be noted for future reference. This need not be a lengthy

document, but should record the type of ware, the extent and type of damage and the cleaning, repair and retouching methods and materials used. It is also a good idea to photograph the object as it is received and at various stages in the repair process. An example of a completed treatment record follows opposite. Often a treatment plan may be made and for many reasons can be altered or amended due to subsequent findings. It is important to record these changes and the reasons for them. A series of tick boxes is a very simple and quick way of recording all the materials used when repairing an object.

Identifying the ceramic body

'Ceramics' is a broad definition for all objects made from fired clay; it comes from the Greek word *keramikos* (of pottery). Clays are formed from the weathering of rocks, and they are composed of many different compounds. There are two types of clays: primary and secondary clays.

Primary clays are formed from the decomposition of feldspar and have not been disturbed by natural elements such as weathering. The purest form of primary clay is known as kaolin, which is often referred to as China or pure clay and is an essential ingredient in the manufacture of real porcelain. Secondary clays are those that have been moved by wind or water and in doing so have gathered many impurities. The properties and vitrification temperature of clays can be changed by the addition of various different components to the clay. It is these additions that result in (broadly speaking) three specific types of ceramic bodies: earthenware, stoneware and porcelain. However, for the purposes of restoration, it is necessary to consider a ceramic body as porous or non-porous. The porosity of the body will determine the type of treatment, especially with regard to cleaning, but also the suitability of applied materials, particularly adhesives.

The firing temperatures needed to change clay into ceramic are, approximately:

800–1000°C (1472–1832°F) for earthenware
1000–1200°C (1832–2192°F) for stoneware
1200–1450°C (2192–2642°F) for porcelain

Treatment Record Form

Name of client	
Address	
Contact telephone numbers	
Date object received	
Estimated time for completion	
Description of object	
Conservation report & desired outcome	

Treatments							Other
Debonding	H_2O	IMS	Acetone	Nitromors	Laponite	H_2O_2/NH_3	
Cleaning	H_2O	bio powder	solvent	steam clean	Laponite	H_2O_2/NH_3	
Rebonding	HMG	B72	5 min epoxy	standard epoxy	special epoxy		
Gap filling	HMG	B72	plaster	standard epoxy	special epoxy		

Replacement of missing parts

Moulding material	latex	steramould	silicon	dental wax		
Modelling material	epoxy	plaster	Milliput			
Retouching	acrylic	epoxy	pigments	porcelain restoration glaze	MSA	
Regilding	oil size	water size	acrylic	gold: powder, transfer, loose	bronze powder	acrylic
Other						

*Figure 3. Magnified section
through:*

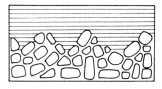

*a. Earthenware body; showing
loose arrangement of clay particles with the glaze 'sitting' on
the body*

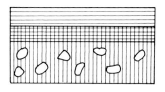

*b. Stoneware body; showing
fewer impurities and fusion
between the glaze and body*

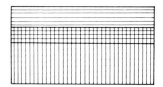

*c. Porcelain body; showing fine
regular structure with complete
fusion of body and glaze*

Every ceramic body has a unique physical and chemical structure. However, a basic understanding of the history and technology of ceramics will help to identify the type of body and accordingly determine its porosity. For example, the Chinese were making a porcellaneous type of stoneware around AD1000, however it was not until some 700 years later that porcelain or 'china' was produced in Great Britain. Therefore, ceramics that were produced in Britain before the 18th century could not be porcelain.

Identifying a body type can often be difficult for an untrained eye. However much can also be learnt by simple examination using a magnifying glass and a pen light. The use of a microscope (suitable for large objects) will also yield interesting information particularly about any glaze and applied decoration.

The thickness and weight of the body are also good indicators of type. For instance, soft-paste porcelain is lighter and less dense than hard-paste. If there is a broken shard or chipped area available for examination this will be particularly useful in identifying the structure and characteristics of the body.

Low-fired earthenwares have a high proportion of impurities (lime and iron oxide). These produce a microscopically rough and 'open' texture which contributes to the porosity of these bodies. Earthenwares require glazing in order to make them impervious to liquids. Often the glaze is only 'loosely' attached to the body making them vulnerable to damage. In their natural state, earthenwares range from grey, through greens, reds and browns, even almost black. The most commonly recognised earthenwares are the red clays or terracottas. Earthenwares are opaque.

Stonewares are generally off-white to brown in colour, heavy and dense. They will give a ringing tone when tapped, although this is less resonant than that given by porcelain, and totally unlike earthenware which sounds dull. Stoneware is roughly textured with a random mix of 'crystals' and some coloured impurities. Stoneware clays are strong, dense, tight, low in porosity and because of the quite similar physical properties of the glazes and bodies, their glazes adhere well. Stonewares are generally considered opaque unless very thinly potted, in which case they may be slightly translucent.

Table 2. Identifying the ceramic body

	Earthenware	Stoneware	Porcelain
	Pottery		
Firing temperature	800–1000°C (1472–1832°F)	1000–1200°C (1832–2192°F)	1200–1450°C (2192–2642°F)
Body characteristics	Porous if not glazed. Non-vitrified. Clay particles loosely arranged.	Partially vitrified. Non-porous. Coarse, granular structure.	Vitrified, fine, close knit and glassy appearance. Ringing note when struck with a fingernail.
Typical body colour	Reddish, terracotta white, off-white.	Beige, sandy/brown white.	Usually white, if thin enough will be translucent if held up to light.
Typical examples	Slipware. Creamware. Pearlware. Tin-glaze:delftware, faience, Maiolica. Unglazed terracotta. Roman pottery. Samian ware. Staffordshire.	Salt glaze. Ironstone china. Jasper ware. Black basalt. Bellarmine. Caneware. Cologne ware. Martin ware. Victorian jam jars. Victorian medicine bottles.	Soft-paste (most early English porcelain up to c.1740). ALSO Hard paste: Chinese export wares Later Parian Worcester, Meissen, Belleek, Sèvres, Bone China
Material suitability for use on:	Porous wares		Non porous wares
Cleaning and dismantling	All, but use any cleaning material with special caution on any porous body		All, but use with caution on any applied decoration, e.g. gilding and overglaze enamels
Bonding	Solvent-based adhesive		All, but do not use low viscosity epoxy resin on soft paste or bone china
Filling	Plaster-based or epoxy on suitably consolidated areas		All
Retouching and gilding	All		All

Notes
- *Always examine the object in good light with magnification*
- *Remember to photograph the object in its damaged state and/or draw an exploded diagram*

Porcelain is a non-porous body with a glassy (vitrified), regular crystalline structure. Hard-paste porcelain is dense, uniformly white, with a close-fitting glaze. Bone china, which is actually a soft-paste type of porcelain, has the same type of dense crystalline structure as hard-paste, although it does exhibit some characteristics of a more porous body, notably in relation to its adverse reaction with low viscosity (thin) adhesives. Bone china gets its name from the addition of bone ash, which accounts for the very white colour that is typical of this type of ceramic body. Porcelain is translucent when held up to the light, although thicker wares may appear opaque.

Different ceramic bodies require different repair methods and materials, and accordingly it is important to know the type of body with which you are dealing. Table 2 is intended to help you identify the correct materials and processes for restoration.

Glossary of ceramic and decorative terms

Further information relating to the identification and description of ceramic bodies is contained in the glossary.

Biscuit or bisque 'Biscuit firing' refers to a once-fired unglazed ceramic body, or the first firing of such a body. Biscuit is a semi-porous, unglazed, very white body with a chalk-like appearance. The break edge will show a granular appearance.

Body The term used to describe the characteristics of specific ceramics, e.g. colour, texture, strength.

Bone china A form of soft-paste porcelain fired high in biscuit and lower in glost. It is highly vitrified (glassy), translucent and very white in appearance. It is called 'bone' china because of the addition of bone ash (calcium phosphate). It is the standard English and American porcelain.

Ceramic From the Greek *keramikes* meaning pottery. Technically, any form of hard, brittle, heat- and corrosion-resistant material, made by firing a non-metallic mineral such as clay. Generally understood nowadays as a collective term to describe all fired clay products.

China clay (kaolin) An essential constituent of hard-paste porcelain.

Chinese export ware Hard-paste porcelain specifically made for export from China for European and American requirements.

Clay A fine-grained, firm earthy material that is plastic when wet and hardens when heated. Widely used for making bricks, tiles and pottery.

Crackle A deliberate cracking of the glaze induced for decorative purposes, often with a stain to make the effect more pronounced.

Crazing An accidental cracking of the glaze, caused by differing range of expansion and contraction between the body and glaze of an object.

Earthenware All pottery that is not vitrified. It was the first type of pottery to be made and it is still very much in use today. Earthenwares are low-fired, opaque, porous, non-vitrified, coarse bodies.

Feldspathic rock A mineral containing silica and alumina, it is one of the most important raw materials used in ceramic manufacture, and also an ingredient in stoneware and porcelain glazes.

Firing The heating of objects in a kiln. Different firing temperatures produce different degrees of hardness, porosity and vitrification.

Firing cracks Cracks that have occurred during firing, distinguishable by their soft melted edges.

Flux A flux can be added to clay bodies to help change the chemical properties of the clay during firing, i.e. giving greater strength and reducing porosity. Flux as a constituent of a glaze helps to reduce the melting point of the materials used in the glaze, thus allowing firing at a lower temperature.

Frit Vitreous materials used in the manufacture of soft-paste porcelain.

Glaze This is the coating applied to a ceramic body. Glazes serve both as practical and decorative finishes. The practical purpose is to reduce porosity, especially in the case of earthenware. There were originally four principal kinds of glazes: feldspathic, tin and salt, which are transparent, and lead, which is opaque. Hard-paste porcelain usually has a feldspathic glaze, soft-paste lead, stoneware salt and earthenware tin. Earthenwares and stonewares are usually decorated in underglaze colours, i.e the body is fired, painted, glazed and refired. Tin glaze is biscuit fired and then coated with a tin glaze, decorated and refired. The addition of tin oxide makes the glaze opaque.

In-glaze decoration – method of decoration onto an unfired glazed surface. This causes the decoration to fuse with the glaze during the glost firing. Maiolica and Delftware are examples of this.

Over-glaze decoration (on-glaze decoration/enamelling) – coloured pigments mixed with a flux which are used for decorating onto previously fired glazed wares; on refiring the pigments fuse with the glaze.

Glost – Glazed state; a glost kiln is one in which the glaze is fired.

Ground Background colour or texture of the surface of an object.

Imari Japanese wares made specifically for export to Europe. These are heavily decorated enamel-glazed wares that were much copied by many English factories in the late 18th century. Produced by Worcester, Chelsea and Spode amongst others.

Impasto Decorative raised glazed patterns using a thick coating of slip.

Kaolin *See* China clay.

Lustreware Metallic surface decoration produced by reduction atmosphere firing.

Opaque A body that does not allow the transmission of light.

Parian Parian is a vitrified form of biscuit porcelain. Most often found in an unglazed form, early Parian is soft-paste, with a silky texture and a slightly translucent, creamy white body capable of showing the most intricate detail. Later Parian is of the hard-paste variety, which was easier to fire but gave a coarse-textured product that did not show the fine detail of earlier Parian. Used extensively for busts and figurines, the production of Parian ceased in the 1890s.

Porcelain The word porcelain is derived from the Portuguese word for a cowrie shell, porcellana. In 1516 the Portuguese explorer Odoardo Barbosa reported that the Chinese used ground-up shell in the manufacture of their translucent wares. China had a tradition of pottery making going back to 1500BC and the first 'true porcelains' were manufactured in China in AD618–907 during the Tang dynasty (and are known as Tang ware). The type of porcelain familiar in the West was first manufactured in China during the Yuan dynasty *c.* AD1297–1368. There are two main types of porcelain:

soft-paste and hard-paste. While their ingredients differ slightly, the terms 'hard' and 'soft' refer chiefly to the different firing temperatures.

Soft-paste ('artificial' porcelain). Semi-vitrified body fired at around 1200°C (2192°F). It was an attempt by the Europeans to imitate the Chinese porcelain that led to the development of soft-paste (or 'artificial') porcelain which was originally ground glass mixed with white clay. Produced in quantity by the Saint Cloud factory near Paris in the 17th century, it is no longer made today. Soft-paste porcelain shows a granular body when chipped. It had to be fired in an unglazed state and then refired at lower (softer) temperatures after glazing. Further firings at low temperatures were also necessary to fix the over-glaze enamel decoration and gilding.

Hard-paste ('true' or 'high-fired' porcelain). This is a highly vitrified form of porcelain that is fired at around 1450°C (2642°F). It gives a ringing tone when tapped, and shows a flint-like fracture when broken. The body and glaze are usually fired in one operation and consequently fuse together. Hard-paste is the standard European porcelain and was first made in China and much later at most of the continental factories, particularly the Meissen factory in France in the 18th century. The body consists of a mixture of kaolin (china clay) and petunse (a feldspathic rock). Hard-paste porcelain was first manufactured in Britain in Plymouth (1768–70) and Bristol (1770–81), but the more common British and American body is the related bone china (see separate entry, previously).

Samian Ware (Red gloss pottery). Roman pottery with a smooth, shiny surface.

Sgraffito Simple form of decorating slipwares by incising a pattern through the slip to reveal the colour underneath.

Slip Slip is clay and water mixed to a creamy consistency, used for decoration (slipware) and casting (slip casting).

Slipwares Earthenwares decorated with slip. Designs were then painted, trailed, or combed on.

Sprigging Form of decoration in which shallow press moulds are used to reproduce motifs, which are then fixed onto the object

Stoneware These wares are hard, non porous, vitreous and opaque. Much more durable body than earthenware.

Bellarmine The English name given to salt glazed stoneware wine bottles that are characterised by a bearded face on the neck of the bottle. Originally made in the 16th century in Germany and copied by John Dwight in England. Also known as greybeards, Cologne ware and Rhenish stoneware.

Black basalt Made by Josiah Wedgwood in the mid 18th century. Its body is stained with oxides of iron and manganese to produce a black vitreous ware that is unglazed though often decorated in gold lustre. Wedgwood used this for his neoclassical designs.

Caneware Also known as bamboo ware, this is a stoneware that was introduced by Wedgwood in the 18th century. Pieces were made to look like bamboo canes.

Cologne ware Stonewares produced between the 15th and 17th centuries in Cologne.

Ironstone A very strong white stoneware that was used for tablewares. Originally made by C.J. Mason in the early 19th century, it is sometimes known as Mason's ironstone.

Jasper ware A very fine vitreous stoneware body, cobalt blue being the most common body colour. Usually found with applied white relief (sprigged) decoration. The most well-known of all the Wedgwood wares

Martin ware A decorative 19th-century salt-glazed stoneware, made by the Martin brothers in London and Southall.

Salt glaze A process whereby common salt is added to the kiln during firing, producing a characteristic 'orange peel' appearance of the glaze.

Vitreous From the Latin vitreus for 'glassy'; applied to ceramic bodies which have a very low porosity due to vitrification caused either by high firing or by the presence of glass particles in the body mix.

3. Cleaning

Before any cleaning processes are embarked upon, some thought should be given as to why the cleaning is being undertaken. Cleaning is an irreversible process, and therefore should not be undertaken lightly. Points that need to be considered are why is the object being cleaned? Is the dirt harmful? What type of dirt is it? Should it be removed or is it part of the history/patina of the object?

The cleaning of any ceramic object should commence only after the initial examination. Investigations and spot tests can then be carried out (i.e. a cotton swab wetted with a small amount of the cleaning solution applied to an inconspicuous area) to establish which cleaning methods and materials should be employed. The cleaning process may involve the removal of loosely attached surface dirt, or greasy or waxy accretions, or the complete dismantling of previous repairs. Other stains may have penetrated the body of the ceramic, such as organic matter like gravy, tea or oil, which may have to be removed with a soaking and/or poulticing process. Inorganic stains such as rust and earth may require more complex cleaning agents.

Cleaning tests should be undertaken methodically and results noted carefully. The basic approach is to employ gentle cleaning agents before moving onto more aggressive substances, in accordance with the list shown below, until an effective method is found.

If you decide that the cleaning procedure you are using is not effective, it is necessary to remove any material residue from the ceramic body before embarking on another cleaning process. This applies to all cleaning situations and materials.

Cleaning agents and processes

1. Distilled or de-ionised water.
2. Non-ionic detergent solution (e.g the 'Fairy' brand of washing-up liquid in water).
3. Biological washing powder (with the addition of a

water softener such as *Calgon*) *Biotex* and *Ariel* are commonly used brands

4. Hydrogen peroxide with a small amount of ammonia solution.
5. Poultices – Laponite, sepiolite, fuller's earth.
6. Solvents – Acetone, industrial methylated spirits, white spirit.

Numbers 1 and 2 are mostly suitable for general cleaning purposes and can be used to wash/soak objects, or for delicate/intricate cleaning with soft brushes. Numbers 3, 4 and 5 are used for stain removal, particularly ingrained organic staining. Number 6 – these are usually used for degreasing and more particularly for removal of old adhesives, infills and over-painting – *use with caution*! In addition to these products, a dichloromethane paint stripper such as *Nitromors* can be used to dismantle previous restorations, particularly epoxy resin adhesives, although it is not a cleaning agent as such.

Few of the materials used for ceramic restoration have been designed specifically for conservation purposes and it must be stressed that no long-term studies have been carried out as to the effects of certain chemicals on ceramic bodies and glazes. Accordingly, it is not completely understood what damage may arise from cleaning agents and other material residues left in the ceramic body. However, it is known that hydrogen peroxide residue incompletely rinsed from objects causes a yellowing of porous ceramics, and has a deleterious effect on certain adhesives – it can stop an epoxy from fully curing. Some constituents of biological washing powders, for example EDTA (ethylene diamine tetra-acetic acid) and *Calgon* (a water softener), may react with iron compounds in earthenware and cause discolouration, and these should therefore be used with caution. The use of chlorine-based bleaches (household bleach) can cause severe damage to the object and should never be used. Abrasive pastes and cleaners should also never be used since they can easily scratch glazes and remove gilding. Porous earthenwares should in general be approached with caution. Some clay objects may be unfired and *will dissolve completely if immersed*!

Always do spot tests before proceeding.

Distilled and de-ionised water

This is preferable to tap water, and can be used safely with a swab or soft brush for gentle removal of surface dirt and dust. Use absorbent tissue to mop up the excess.

Non-ionic detergent solution

Use the detergent in solution with distilled water. It can then be applied by a swab (roll some cotton wool around a cocktail stick) to clean the ceramic body. For high-fired wares this can be diluted by the addition of up to 50% of white spirit and the resultant solution shaken to form an emulsion which can then be used as a degreasing agent. This emulsion can be used for wet washing, but complete immersion is not recommended.

Biological washing powders

Cleaning Presoak all ceramics in clean, cold water before starting any cleaning using washing powder. A solution made with a tablespoon each of *Calgon* and *Biotex* in about 5 litres (approx. 1½ gallons) of water can be used to immerse ceramics (complete or broken) with organic stains (tea, coffee, gravy, wine, oil etc.) which should then be left to soak for up to twelve hours.

Cleaning an object with a soft toothbrush

Monitor progress carefully every twenty minutes for the first hour or two, then every couple of hours thereafter, checking that there are no adverse reactions. The solution should be changed as required and the pieces washed in clean, gently running warm water when renewing the detergent solution. Take care when leaving ceramics in running water to avoid further damage. It is not necessary to use hot water as modern enzyme detergents are capable of working at temperatures as low as 10°C (50°F), and enzymes may become inactive at temperatures above 40°C (104°F).

A more concentrated solution, consisting of one tablespoon each of *Calgon* and *Biotex* (or *Ariel* on its own) in a litre (2 pt) of warm water can be applied on cotton wool to an area of staining – on the bottom of a gravy boat for example – and the progress monitored. Rubbing gently with a soft toothbrush or stencil brush may assist here.

Where it is undesirable to clean an entire object (e.g. friable surfaces or vulnerable over-glaze decoration) biological powder can be mixed with a little de-ionised water to form a thick paste, this can then be applied to the specific area and used in the same way as a poultice (see below).

Rinsing procedure When the pieces have been cleaned to a satisfactory state, they should then be left to soak for a few days in frequently changed clean (if possible, de-ionised/distilled) cold water to make sure all traces of washing powder are removed.

Drying procedure After rinsing thoroughly place the object on an absorbent surface, e.g. a clean dish towel, blotting paper or kitchen roll. Leave it in a warm room and allow the object to dry out completely. Cover with absorbent material to prevent dust sticking to it.

If the biological powder process is not working and you decide to switch to hydrogen peroxide, it will be necessary to follow the prescribed rinsing procedure described above before any change of cleaning materials can be made. *Never mix cleaning processes.*

Note: while vitrified bodies (porcelain) may dry in one or two days, porous bodies are best left for up to a month or so to dry out completely. Where possible, weighing an object before cleaning and periodically during the drying process can be a useful exercise. When the object returns to its original weight it can then be considered dry and ready for further treatment where necessary.

Hydrogen peroxide

Peroxide comes in volume strengths (20, 40, 60), and depending on the type of stain it may be used either diluted with water or undiluted. Add to the peroxide one or two drops of ammonia (.880) solution. The ammonia solution acts as a catalyst, i.e. it speeds up the action of the hydrogen peroxide. This cleaning agent may not be suitable for use on white earthenwares because it may cause discolouration of the body. The peroxide must *never* be applied directly to a dry piece as this will only fix the stain permanently by drawing it into the ceramic body.

Soak the object for two hours in cold water and apply the peroxide solution on cotton wool swabs. Wrap in clingfilm. Apply more solution with a pipette or dropper to the swabs frequently and make sure that the swabs are not allowed to dry out. When the stains have been removed, soak in several changes of clean cold water and dry thoroughly as previously described.

If the stains seem to be particularly stubborn the strength of the peroxide solution may be increased by using a greater volume of peroxide to a lesser volume of water. Placing the object in an appropriate solvent-proof container in the dark will help to speed up the action of the peroxide. In extreme cases, stoneware and porcelain can be soaked in an undiluted solution but great care should be taken and the process monitored closely.

Poultice methods of cleaning

These involve using a material which, as it dries, draws out stains from the ceramic body.

Laponite is a synthetic clay which is used as a poulticing agent to remove grease, old adhesive and stains from various materials including ceramics. The object must be presoaked in cold water for about two hours before applying the Laponite. The Laponite is mixed with water in a 5% solution (this is roughly 2 tablespoons to 1 litre (approx. 2 pt of water), and allowed to stand for about two hours, during which time the solution becomes a thick gel. The gel should be regularly stirred to avoid the formation of any lumps. The standing time

Spreading laponite over the crack

may be reduced by using warm water.

The gel is then spread over the stained area to a thickness of 3–4mm (approx.⅛in.), and the object covered loosely with clingfilm and allowed to stand. The clingfilm prevents the Laponite from drying out too quickly, which is important since the substance works by drawing the stain out gradually during the drying out process. After two to three days the clingfilm can be removed and the Laponite allowed to dry until it is firm but not hard (up to another three days although the time will be dependent on the temperature and relative humidity of the environment). The poultice should then be removed and the object washed. This process may need to be repeated several times until the object has been satisfactorily cleaned. In the case of an object with a crazed glaze, once it has been ascertained that there is no instability such as a friable surface, the Laponite should be applied over the whole object to prevent uneven cleaning.

When dealing with organic stains (e.g. on meat plates, etc.) the object can be soaked first in a detergent solution, rinsed, and soaked in cold water before applying the Laponite. A small quantity of white spirit or industrial methylated spirit may be added to the

Laponite gel to assist the removal of oily organic stains. Alternatively, a small quantity of hydrogen peroxide and ammonia solution can be added to the Laponite – this will have a bleaching effect on the stains. Once dry, the Laponite becomes almost impossible to remove from an object. It is therefore necessary to ensure that it is completely removed before it has had a chance to dry out totally.

Fullers earth and Sepiolite These are used in exactly the same way as Laponite, although they form a paste rather than a gel when mixed with water.

Blotting paper can also be 'pulped' with a small amount of water in a food blender, and used effectively and more cheaply as a poulticing agent using exactly the same method as above.

Solvents

These are generally used to soften previous restoration materials before removal, and to degrease break edges prior to rebonding. See section on dismantling previous restorations (pp. 37–38).

Metal stain removal

Rivets and metal dowels as well as any corroded metal that comes into contact with a ceramic body may cause inorganic staining. These stains cannot be removed with detergents or oxidising agents such as hydrogen peroxide, but require the use of rust converters. One such product is *Jenolite*, a form of phosphoric acid that works by converting the rust (iron oxide) to iron phosphate which can then be more easily removed from the object.

Jenolite gel should be applied to the metal stain and left for fifteen to twenty minutes, after which time it can be washed off and applied again until an acceptable level of cleaning has been achieved. As with all cleaning procedures, progress should be monitored closely. After this, follow the prescribed rinsing and drying procedure, ensuring that all traces of the Jenolite are completely removed. Any Jenolite residue left on the object can affect the setting of epoxy resin adhesive.

Other compounds, which may remove rust stains and/or encrustations from objects are EDTA, sodium hydrogen sulphate, citric acid, and oxalic acid. These are available from chemical suppliers and need to be dissolved in water before use. As with all cleaning procedures, start off by applying a test swab of a weak solution. The concentration of the solutions may be increased until the desired strength is found. As always, objects must be thoroughly rinsed to ensure complete removal of any chemical residues.

Steam cleaning

Recently the use of a steam cleaner has proved to be a very effective and quick method of cleaning, and sometimes, depending on the adhesive used, it is also a good method of dismantling an object.

Steam cleaning units are small – they will sit on a worktop and deliver steam under pressure from a hand-held directional nozzle. This provides for the easy cleaning of ingrained dirt from cracks, crevices, and textured surfaces. Cleaning is thorough, quick and efficient. It does not over-wet the object and it often negates the need for other cleaning processes, especially those involving chemicals. Dirty water should be wiped away as it is produced, using a clean absorbent swab. Although expensive, these units have great benefits in terms of health and safety and they often allow an object to be cleaned without the need for soaking.

However, as with all cleaning procedures, care must be taken. Steam cleaning should not be used in areas of apparent fragility, such as friable surfaces, over-glaze enamels and gilding. Gilding, even when fired, can sometimes easily be accidentally removed with the steam cleaner.

Dry cleaning

For some ceramics which are not suitable for wetting it may be possible to remove surface dirt with a material called 'draught clean powder' (pulverised soya bean fibre with calcium hydroxide) which is available 'loose' or sewn into a cotton 'pad'. The powder is gently rubbed over the surface with a brush or soft, lint-free cloth. The pad is used in the same way but without the brush or cloth. This method may remove surface dirt, but it is generally a slow process.

A specialist putty eraser (available from art shops) may also be used to gently rub off dirty marks if they are not completely ingrained in the porous ceramic. Only the clean areas of the rubber should be used for removal of contaminants. Dirty areas should not be re-used as they may re-introduce contaminants back onto the surface of the object.

Note: *do not use dry cleaning methods on friable surfaces!*

Indirect application of solvents

Sometimes it may be necessary to use a solvent but it is not possible to apply the solvent directly to the object, e.g. old adhesive on a porous body, where an initial test may show that the solvent will cause irreversible staining. If this is the case, place the object inside a solvent-proof container together with the solvent – placed in a smaller, separate open-topped container – and cover the outer container with a tight fitting lid. Once contained the local atmosphere becomes saturated with solvent fumes and these fumes should 'undo' the old adhesive. This method is efficient with solvent-based adhesives and will work with epoxy resin, but will often take time

Note: *Great care must be taken when removing the lid, because there will be a rush of evaporating solvent. Ensure that appropriate precautions are taken to prevent the inhalation of fumes. Wear a mask and goggles.*

Dismantling previous restorations

Adhesives

All organic and animal-based glues can usually be removed with warm or hot water. Start by using a wetted swab and apply to the affected area, which should establish if the adhesive is removable with water. If after several minutes the glue is beginning to break down, then the piece can be immersed in hand-hot water (provided the object is suitable for immersion) to soften the old adhesive. However, if after several minutes the glue does not appear to be softening, it is possible that the adhesive is a synthetic one.

Synthetic adhesives (not epoxies) can often be broken down with acetone, industrial methylated spirits, or white spirit. Using a swab wetted with one of these

Figure 4.

a Right angle rivet

b Acute angle rivet. Rivets imbedded at this angle will often need to be cut through before removal.

Figure 5.

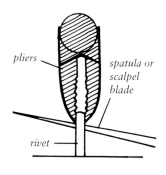

pliers

spatula or scalpel blade

rivet

solvents should establish whether the adhesive is soluble. The solvent can then be applied onto long cotton wool rolls about 1 cm (½ in.) in diameter and laid along the old adhesive break edge. The object can be covered with clingfilm to slow down the rate of evaporation of the solvent.

If the glue initially shows no sign of softening, this process can be repeated until the glue is sufficiently soft to allow the object to be easily dismantled

If the solvent procedure is not working, wash the object and dry thoroughly. Using a suitable small brush apply water-based Nitromors to the old adhesive and break line; then cover the whole object or area with clingfilm which will support the object and prevent complete collapse of the pieces. Monitor the process periodically. When satisfied that the adhesive is softening and breaking down, remove the clingfilm and wipe off excess with disposable kitchen towel, wearing heavy-duty domestic rubber gloves. Then place the object in a plastic basin containing cold water. *Follow the procedure in a very well-ventilated area, or preferably in an extraction booth since fumes given off can cause respiratory problems.*

Nitromors will not dissolve an epoxy resin, but it will soften it. Therefore several applications may be necessary to ensure the complete dismantling of an object. It may also be necessary to apply more Nitromors to the break edges in order to remove any remaining adhesive. Any remaining residues can be removed using a scalpel or pin (held in a pin vice) and by gently scrubbing with a toothbrush or stencil brush. Use a combination of these tools and methods to remove *all* trace of adhesive.

When all the old adhesive has been removed, wash in several changes of clean water and leave in a warm place on absorbent material (tea towel), properly supported (on a tray or plastic container) and protected from dust. When dry, examine edges carefully in a side light – any old adhesive will show up in the light. This should then be removed mechanically, or by the application of more solvent.

Rivets

For many years the preferred method of mending ceramics was by rivetting, i.e. joining the shards together by using wire staples that were fixed into holes

A sketch diagram

Your sketch diagram need not be a work of art, but it can be a useful and simple way of recording an object and any missing or damaged areas.

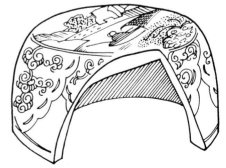

Figure 7.

Rivet sawn in half

Figure 8.

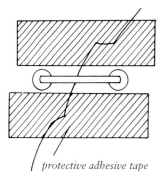

protective adhesive tape

drilled into the ceramic. Rivetting, properly done, was a very skilled craft, however it is not one that is used today because of the irreversible damage that is caused to the ceramic by the need to drill holes all over it.

It may not always be necessary (or desirable) to remove metal repairs. It may, for instance, be decided that they are an intrinsic part of the object's history and that they should be left in place. However, where they have become unstable or are causing staining or damage to the ceramic body, it is usually desirable to remove them. Great care must be taken not to cause further damage to the object during removal of the rivets.

When a decision has been taken to remove metal repairs on ceramics, it is necessary to assess how the repair was originally carried out, to enable removal without damage to the body. Right angle rivets are usually easier to remove than acute angle rivets. The ends of the metal rivet are usually embedded in a plaster-filled hole. The plaster can be softened by applying a wet cotton swab and then carefully removed with the tip of a scalpel blade (number 11), dental probe, or fine metal point (*wear goggles*). This should facilitate the removal of the rivets, particularly right angle rivets. The end of a spatula can then be gently eased under the rivet which is prised up carefully, or a small pair of blunt nosed pliers or forceps can be used to pull it out (see Figure 5, p.58).

Occasionally metal rivets are lead-soldered onto the ceramic. In this case a soldering iron should be carefully employed to soften the solder, enabling the rivet to be removed.

To remove other metal wire repairs such as 'lacing' it may be necessary to cut through the wire and tease out the metal ties with a small pair of pliers or forceps. It may not be possible to cut through some iron repairs with pliers, and therefore when absolutely necessary, a fine small hacksaw blade may be employed. This method may often be necessary when removing acute angle rivets as well.

Mask off the surrounding area on either side of the rivet with masking tape to prevent damage to the ceramic, and proceed with great caution. Use the hacksaw blade with extreme caution to saw through the middle of the rivet and remove each half separately.

Judiciously placed small pieces of adhesive tape will hold the pieces of the object together, and prevent them falling apart when the rivets are removed. The tape also helps to protect the surface of the object when using a hacksaw blade (Figure 8). Any rivet holes must be thoroughly cleaned of any remaining debris, using a metal stain remover (see p. 35) if necessary.

Notes
- *Only immerse non-porous wares that are stable and non-friable*
- *Clean all soft-bodied wares separately to avoid cross-contamination*
- *Pre-soak in (preferably) de-ionised cold water to prevent stains being drawn into the body, but never allow the object to soak in dirty solutions*
- *Take care when ceramics are being rinsed*
- *Note that large, soft-bodied wares may take a month or more to dry completely if they have been immersed during cleaning*
- *Remember that the final appearance of any cleaned object is often not apparent until complete drying has taken place*
- *Crazed or weathered glazes are more at risk during the cleaning process, and on-glaze decoration is more vulnerable than under-glaze decoration*
- *Check that any gilding has been fired and is stable before embarking on any cleaning procedure*

4. Bonding

Many diverse materials have been used in the past to repair broken ceramics. These include precious metals such as gold, used in ancient times to stick shards together and fill gaps, to later rivetted repairs using lead, iron and copper rivets or 'staples'. This type of repair has been used extensively, and although aesthetically disfiguring, ethically any particularly well-executed repairs should be retained as long as they are stable and not causing damage or staining to the ceramic body.

Adhesives have a long history. The earliest repairs used sticky organic matter, including such materials as gelatin, isinglass, egg, cheese and other animal products. An example from the day-book of George Nathan Maynard, curator of Saffron Walden museum 1880–1904:

> Powder of Suffolk cheese dried powdered and sifted, unslaked lime in powder. Mix equal parts with hard water, cold on a slab till stringy. It is then ready for use. Put on each side of the broken edges and hold before the fire till it sets and in five hours it is done. N.B. the more cheese the stronger it is. Boil the cheese to get the fat out. (sic)

One such material, which was once in common usage, is shellac, a sticky resin, excreted by insects. Dissolved in alcohol, it was used as an adhesive. It is now seldom used for this purpose, but it may be employed as a surface coating on plaster fills. Unbleached shellac is usually brownish in colour and may cause staining to the ceramic body.

Cellulose nitrate adhesives (popularly known as HMG, balsa wood glue or Airfix kit adhesive) have been in use since the 19th century, and continue to be used widely in ceramic repair, partly due to the ease with which they may be removed. They dry by evaporation of solvent, so that adding a solvent to the dry adhesive will 'undo' the glue. Acetone is usually used for this purpose.

Paraloid B72 (co-polymer of methyl acrylate and ethyl

methacrylate) is another adhesive, which works by solvent evaporation, and one that was especially developed for the conservation profession. It is durable and non-yellowing, available in a tube and in granular form. The granules need to be mixed with a solvent before use (usually acetone). Paraloid can be used both as an adhesive and also as a consolidant.

Epoxy adhesives – although technically irreversible, epoxies are widely used for high-fired wares. A common brand employed for rebonding ceramics is *Araldite*. There are also some epoxies, which have been developed specifically for use on porcelain and glass, these are: *Hxtal NYL-1*, *Fynebond* and *Araldite 2020*.

Instant glues (cynoacrylates), although marketed as an instant cure-all, have caused many problems due to their misuse. They do have a limited use for tacking shards together or for holding small shards in place until a more permanent adhesive is applied over the cynoacrylates, but it is not advisable to use *any* fast setting adhesives until you are conversant with sticking order, alignment of shards, and the general methodology of ceramic repair. A lot of damage may be caused by the unwitting use of such adhesives. These types of adhesives are known to degrade in time and they are very brittle. It is also thought that they will lose strength on prolonged exposure to light, and degrade severely in alkaline conditions. They should not be used as a permanent rebonding solution.

Adhesive selection

After identifying and cleaning the piece, the next stage in the repair process is bonding. Before this can actually be done the correct adhesive must be selected, and you will need to consider the following criteria when making your choice.

1. Suitability/compatibility The adhesive chosen should be compatible with the type of ceramic. In general, those which dry by solvent evaporation are suitable for more porous bodies (e.g. earthenware), whilst for less porous bodies (e.g. porcelain) an epoxy resin, which sets by chemical reaction, should be chosen. It is inadvisable to use a low-viscosity epoxy resin on bone china and soft-paste porcelain, due to an adverse reaction between the adhesive and ceramic body. This type of adhesive can cause the break edges to show as dark lines.

2. Reversibility Any adhesive should be removable without causing damage to the object. While this situation is an ideal, in practice it is often difficult to achieve. Adhesives such as cellulose nitrate and Paraloid B72 dry by evaporation of solvent, and this process can be reversed using that same solvent (usually acetone). Epoxy resins set by chemical reaction and although theoretically irreversible can in practice be softened with an epoxy resin disintegrator (dichlormethane, commonly available as Nitromors paint stripper – use the water-washable type). Complete removal will need to be undertaken mechanically using tools such as scalpels and pins.

Table 3. The physical properties of adhesives

Product name	Viscosity	Tack time/ complete set	Use as a filling material
HMG Cellulose Nitrate	Medium	2/3 min/42 hours	No
Paraloid B-72	Medium	15 min/up to 7 days	Possible
Devcon 5-min Epoxy	High	4min/N/A	No
Araldite Rapid	High	5 min/90 min	No
Araldite Precision	High	90 min/10 hours	Yes
Hxtal NYL-1	Low	72 hours/7 days	Yes
Fynebond	Low	N/A/36–48 hours	Yes
Araldite 20/20	Low	45 mins/25 hours	Yes
Araldite AY103/HY956	Low	90 min/24 hours***	Use as a casting resin

Note: *Cellulose nitrate and Paraloid are solution adhesives, these dry by evaporation of solvent. All other products are reaction adhesives, these set by chemical reaction. The over catalysing of any epoxy will accelerate any yellowing tendencies.*

3. Physical properties

a *Colour* – the ideal adhesive will be water-white, i.e. clear and colourless, and will not discolour over time (see p.47 for more detailed information).

b *Viscosity* – the extent to which a liquid resists flow. A high viscosity adhesive is thick and does not run easily; this is more suitable for an edge-to-edge stick, and this type of adhesive is advised for porous bodies. Low viscosity (thin) adhesives flow freely and are more suitable for dry stick repairs, in which the adhesive is allowed to infiltrate the breaks. It is possible to dilute some adhesives with solvent to make them flow more easily, for example acetone will dilute cellulose nitrate and Paraloid B72. The diluted adhesive can then be used to flow into break edges or run into cracks on earthenwares, although this method of using these adhesives is not recommended.

c *Setting time* – adhesives fall roughly into two cate-

Compatability with ceramic body	Reversability wet/dry	Mixing ratio	Health and safety
All	Acetone/acetone	N/A	Highly flammable
All	Acetone/acetone	** see below	Highly flammable
Non-porous bodies	Acetone/Nitromors	50:50	Irritant
Non-porous bodies	Acetone/Nitromors	50:50	Irritant
Non-porous bodies	Acetone/Nitromors	50:50	Irritant
Non-porous bodies*	Acetone/Nitromors	100:30	Irritant
Non-porous bodies*	Acetone/Nitromors	100:32	Irritant
Non-porous bodies*	Acetone/Nitromors	100:30	Irritant
Not recommended for bonding	Acetone/Nitromors	100:18	Irritant

* not recommended for use on soft-paste porcelain or bone china as an adhesive.
** Paraloid B-72 granules can be used to make a 'tailor-made' solution. See p.48.
*** to ensure complete curing this product must be kept at a constant temperature of -25°C for 24 hours. High relative humidity will adversely affect curing.

gories: the quick setting and the slow setting. By using a quick setting adhesive (but not an instant glue) it is possible to hold the pieces together by hand until the glue is set. This is not possible using a slow setting adhesive and some way must be found to keep the pieces together until the glue is set. This is usually done by using sticky tape, rubber bands or clamps. However, it should be remembered that some surface decoration (e.g. gilding, overglaze enamels) can be damaged by the removal of tape. Tape should not be placed on friable or gilded surfaces.

d *Strength and durability* – these are usually not a problem with modern adhesives, which tend if anything to be *too* strong.

e *Toxicity* – handling epoxy resins can sometimes cause contact dermatitis (skin sensitivity) so that disposable gloves may be advisable. Eyes can also be affected, and accordingly great care should be taken to avoid hand/eye contact. Avoid breathing in resin dust when rubbing down fillings etc. because this may cause respiratory irritation; use a dust mask.

Most adhesives are not overly toxic but care must always be taken when handling any product of this type. *Always read labels and follow manufacturer's instructions carefully.*

4. Ease of handling and mixing Some adhesives can be squeezed directly from the tube onto a palette without mixing. Others need to be premixed by squeezing an equal quantity of resin and hardener onto a mixing pad, white ceramic or melinex (mylar) covered tile or artists' palette, and blending thoroughly. Others (e.g. *Fynebond*) must be weighed out using an accurate scale that weighs in very small gradations, i.e. 0.1g. It is never advisable to apply adhesive straight from the tube.

5. Availability and cost Some adhesives are readily available from hardware, DIY, or artists' supply shops. Most of these are reasonably priced and easy to obtain. Other adhesives may be available only from specialist shops or by mail order, these will also be comparatively expensive. However, although the initial outlay may sometimes be considerable, it is important to remember that adhesives are used sparingly, and you will only need to purchase them occasionally. (See suppliers' lists on p.117 for details of where to purchase adhesives.)

6. Colour stability Many adhesives start off water-white, but unfortunately some adhesives not specifically made for conservation may discolour in time due to the effect of ultraviolet light. In time this discolouration will become more pronounced. It is possible to counteract this to an extent by the addition of a whitening agent (e.g. titanium dioxide, or zinc white pigment), this should be added to the adhesive and blended thoroughly to ensure there are no lumps. Titanium white (and several other colours are available as epoxy paste) these can be used to colour the resin.

Table 3 summarises the adhesives used for ceramic repair and their criteria for selection.

Consolidation

Consolidate means to reinforce, or to strengthen.

Sometimes some ceramics may have areas that are friable, i.e. crumbly or flaking areas or edges. This is more common in porous bodies and in over-glaze enamels. These damaged areas or break edges of these wares will need to be consolidated before any repair process can be started.

Painting a consolidation solution of 10% Paraloid B-72 in acetone onto friable overglaze enamels

A solution of Paraloid B-72 diluted with acetone to make a 5% weight by volume (w/v) or 10% w/v solution is used for this purpose. The stronger (10%) solution should be used in instances of greater damage.

To make a 5% w/v solution: dissolve 5 g (approx. ⅙ oz) of Paraloid B-72 in 95ml (3.34 fl. oz) of acetone.

To make a 10% w/v solution: dissolve 10 g (approx. ⅓ oz) of Paraloid B-72 in 90ml (3.17 fl. oz) of acetone.

The solution is then gently painted or pipetted over the damaged area or break edges using a sable brush or small plastic pipette. More than one coat may need to be applied to very badly flaking or crumbling areas. This solution can also be used to strengthen plaster fills and any replacement parts made of plaster (e.g. handles and knobs etc.) or to seal these prior to retouching. The solution is applied in exactly the same way as described above (i.e. painted or pipetted on). Where a replacement part has been made it is possible to immerse the entire part in a 5% solution to consolidate it. The part should be immersed until the air bubbles have stopped rising to the surface, the piece should then be removed and allowed to dry. In all cases allow twenty-four hours for the solution to dry.

Using Paraloid B-72 as an adhesive

To make a bonding solution of Paraloid B-72:

The Koob recipe

Ingredients
100g of acetone (weigh the acetone, 100g is **not** the same as 100ml)
+ 1tsp fumed silica
+ 50g of B-72 resin granules.

Method
Use a wide mouthed jar (jam jar perhaps), weigh the jar, and record the weight.
Pour the acetone and fumed silica into the jar. Wrap the 50 g of B-72 granules into a gauze cloth, tie with string and suspend this cloth in the jar of acetone, allow it to just touch the acetone. Place a layer of clingfilm over the top of the jar, put the lid on and set it aside to allow the Paraloid B-72 granules to dissolve. **Do not agitate.**

Once all the resin has dissolved remove the lid of the jar, string, and the empty bag, then weigh the jar and contents. Swirl the mixture around, stand the jar in an appropriate spot such as in a fume cupboard or under a fume hood and allow some of solvent to evaporate, check on the weight, and swirl the mixture around from time to time (about every 1–2 hours). Once the mixture has lost 45g in weight (i.e. 45g of acetone has evaporated), replace the clingfilm and lid, and allow the solution to stand until all the air bubbles disappear.

The adhesive is now ready to use. For ease of application it can be poured into aluminium or tin tubes (which are available from artists' supply shops). During pouring, do not leave the solution uncovered for any longer than is absolutely necessary – this will ensure that solvent evaporation is kept to a minimum. Fold the ends of the tubes over using needle nosed pliers, label, date, and store tubes upright until required.

Bonding

The two basic methods of bonding objects are the dry stick and the edge-to-edge stick. Table 4 (p.50) explains which adhesives are recommended for each of these methods. All break edges, *except those previously consolidated*, should be wiped with a cotton swab dipped in acetone immediately prior to rebonding, this will ensure a good clean break edge free of any grease which may inadvertently been transferred from fingers onto the break edges. It is for this reason that the wearing of latex or nitrile gloves is recommended.

1. The dry stick method

This is a method of repair in which the shards are taped together and a low viscosity (very liquid) adhesive is applied in small beads along the break lines on one or both sides of the object. This method is mainly suitable for high-fired wares, i.e. vitreous ceramics, stoneware, porcelain and glass. Although it may be used with glazed earthenwares it is not recommended, but if used, several applications may be needed.

The adhesive is drawn into the break lines and spreads by capillary action, i.e. the beads of adhesive run into the cracks and are attracted to one another; this attraction causes the adhesive to spread along the cracks

---

Table 4. *Adhesives for edge-to-edge and dry sticking*

	Edge-to-edge	Dry stick
Earthenwares	cellulose nitrate Paraloid B-72	Not recommended
Stonewares	cellulose nitrate Paraloid B-72 Devcon 5-min Epoxy Araldite rapid Araldite Precision	Araldite Precision Araldite 2020 Hxtal NYL–1 Fynebond
Porcelain	cellulose nitrate Paraloid B-72 Devcon 5-min Epoxy Araldite rapid Araldite Precision	Araldite Precision Araldite 2020 Hxtal NYL–1 Fynebond

---

as each bead joins up with the next. It is very important that break edges are as close as possible together, and this can be achieved by stretching magic tape across the join. Be careful not to misalign shards when applying tape. Check by running a fingernail across.

The low viscosity adhesives such as Fynebond or Araldite 2020 etc. are the preferred options to use when dry sticking. They are specialist adhesives that have specific mixing requirements, i.e. they need to be weighed out on a fine balance or carefully measured out by volume using a small pipette.

It is possible to use thicker adhesives that do not have such particular mixing requirements (e.g. Araldite Precision). Apply all along the break edges and gently warm with a hair dryer, and as the adhesive becomes less viscous it will flow between the break edges. Paraloid or cellulose nitrate may be diluted in acetone until they are sufficiently liquid to use to drystick glazed earthenwares. This solution should not be warmed with a hair dryer. The excess may be removed with a slightly wetted acetone swab.

Before applying any adhesive tape check that it will not cause damage to the surface glaze or decoration (i.e. gilding or onglaze enamels). If it is not possible to use adhesive tape or any other support method, such as rubber bands or clamps, then there will be no alternative

Opposite: tea bowl from the Tex-sing cargo before and after bonding – the shard was taped into place using magic tape and Fynebond was infiltrated into the crack. No further work was carried out

other than to use a fast-setting adhesive and hold the pieces together on the workbench until the adhesive has cured.

Low viscosity epoxy resins such as Fynebond should not be used on high-fired wares that have a cracked glaze. This will creep under the surface of the glaze adjacent to the break edges causing a 'river' mark.

The drawing below clarifies the following steps:

- Lay the shards out jigsaw fashion to establish the correct sticking order, and number the pieces using labels made of masking tape (a)
- Use magic tape to fix the shards together carefully, stretching the tape across the joins to ensure a tight fit (b and c)
- Apply beads of adhesive with a cocktail stick onto the break line, at 1cm (½in.) intervals (d)
- Place the object where it will not be disturbed and cover with clingfilm to protect it from dust while drying
- Pare off excess adhesive with a scalpel before fully set
- Remove tape and any further remaining adhesive

Bonding a multi-break plate using the dry stick method:
a Shards laid out jigsaw fashion and labelled in sticking order
b Shards taped together carefully
c Object ready for sticking
d Adhesive applied in small beads along the joins

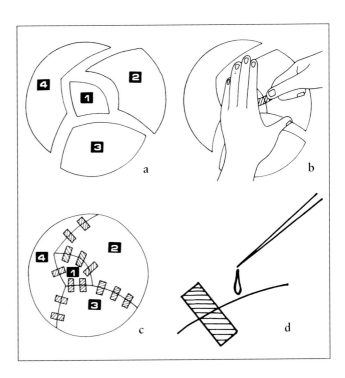

Shards of a porcelain charger laid out jigsaw fashion, ready for taping

Below: shards taped together ready for dry sticking

a

b

Above: Using a fast setting adhesive
a Small dots of adhesive applied to break edge with cocktail stick
b Edges aligned and held firmly until adhesive has set

Above: Using rubber bands to support a cup handle until the adhesive has set

2. The edge-to-edge stick method

This is a method in which the adhesive is applied onto the break edges, and the two edges are then brought together and held firmly until the adhesive has set. This is done in one of two ways:

a By using fast-setting adhesive (as above.)
b By using a slow-setting adhesive and supporting the object, ensuring there is no movement whatsoever until the adhesive has set. Rubber bands are very useful for this purpose, but care needs to be taken that they are placed in the correct position, or the two pieces will slip apart. You may need several 'dry' runs to get the positioning right.

For both methods, de-grease the break edges of your object with acetone swabs, ensuring no cotton fibres are left on the ceramic.
Warning: too much adhesive will cause the misalignment of shards.

Bonding a wedge-shaped break

P. 56 (top) shows a common wedge-shaped break where

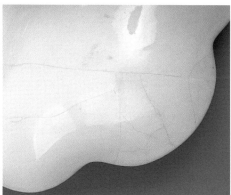

the shards of a plate are chamfered (broken at an angle). The shards must be inserted simultaneously otherwise they will not fit, and each shard will cause the other to be 'locked out'. Either the edge-to-edge stick or the dry stick method are suitable for this type of repair.

Trials must be undertaken to ascertain at what angle the break edges fit properly together, but take care dur-

Top: earthenware dish rebonded using the 'edge to edge' method with a 50% solution of Paraloid B-72 in acetone
Above left: detail of the back of the dish
Above right: applying Fynebond to the crack

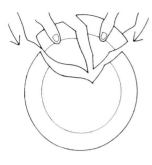

Shards are inserted simultaneously for a wedge-shaped break, either with adhesive already applied, for the edge-to-edge stick method, or to be taped for a dry stick

ing trial runs to avoid causing further damage to the glaze at the break edges, where it can easily chip.

Springing

Sometimes it is not possible to re-align shards as perfectly as desired. This is generally only a problem with high-fired wares, where the high temperatures used to fire the clay and cause vitrification create internal tensions and torque. When broken, these tensions relax and distort the original shape – this is known as springing. It is sometimes possible with specialist clamps to pull these fragments back into alignment. However, the use of any degree of excessive force will often just result in further damage. This method of re-alignment is not advisable to the less experienced conservator. Sometimes, the only option is to accept this situation and try to work around it (see diagram below).

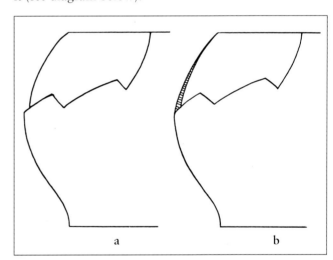

Springing
a Diagram of rebonded object showing step (exaggerated)
b Fill shaped to accommodate step and create a flush surface

Sealing cracks

A low-viscosity adhesive is useful for sealing clean cracks in high-fired wares. The adhesive should be mixed according to the manufacturer's instructions and applied along the crack line with a cocktail stick. Allow approximately fifteen to thirty minutes for the adhesive to penetrate the crack, after which time excess adhesive should be removed using a cotton swab dipped in acetone. Magic tape should then be applied tightly across the crack, to pull the break edges together.

Lay the object gently on its side either in a tray filled

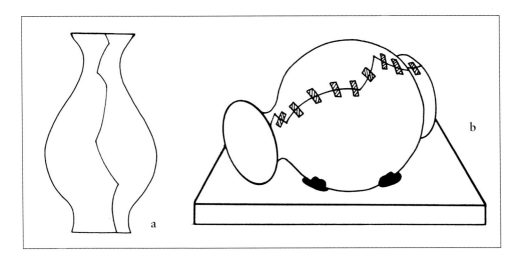

with polystyrene (styrofoam) balls or supported with plasticine or bags of salt. Remove the tape when the adhesive has set and clean the object of any residue.

Note: Be sure to distinguish between cracks caused by mechanical damage and firing cracks. The latter are distinguishable because the glaze will have pooled around the edges of a firing crack giving a soft rounded edge. Those cracks that have occurred after firing will have sharp edges with the glaze ending abruptly.

Sealing cracks
a Vase with a clean vertical crack
b Vase, sealed with adhesive and tape, supported on its side

Notes

- *Always ensure you have an adequate working space so that you can sit comfortably and place the object securely on your work bench*
- *Prepare your working area to ensure you have to hand all necessary equipment and materials, specifically clamping accessories, rubber bands, adhesive tape, mixing tile and spatulas*
- *Before applying adhesive tape always ensure that decoration will not be damaged*
- *Always make a trial run without adhesive. Do not apply adhesive until you have established the correct sticking order*
- *Always select your adhesive according to the type of ware, its decoration and difficulty of repair; remember that epoxy resins should not be used on porous wares, i.e.earthenwares or soft-paste porcelain (including bone china), but may be used on non-porous wares*

5. Filling, casting, modelling & moulding

Filling and casting

When your shards have been bonded, the next stage is to fill in any missing areas. For small areas it is usually easier to fill the gap freehand, using tape or plasticine to support the fill until it is set. For more complicated shapes it may be possible to fill areas by taking an impression and casting missing parts with a liquid fill.

Suitable filling and casting materials are based on plaster and the same epoxy resins that are used for bonding objects. These both have very different properties but both are suitable for a variety of applications. Plaster-based products are suitable for any type of body, while it is preferable to use epoxy resins on non-porous bodies. If using an epoxy fill on a porous body it is essential to ensure that the area to be treated has been properly consolidated before any application of an epoxy fill. It is not recommended to cast epoxy resin onto a porous body.

Using epoxy resins to fill and cast

Araldite 2020, Hxtal NYL-1, and Fynebond when mixed with bulking agents and dry pigments and/or epoxy resin paste colours can also be used to create a fill or cast on all types of low porous wares – these can be exactly matched to the original ceramic. These low viscosity optically clear resins are ideal for making translucent fills.

These resins when suitably bulked are also appropriate for making fills on some of the more stable porous bodies, providing the area of the object to be filled is suitably consolidated, usually with a 5–10% solution of Paraloid B-72 in acetone.

A high viscosity resin such as Araldite Precision is also suitable for use as a coloured filler on opaque wares (providing the slightly yellowish tinge often found in these type of resins does not interfere with the effect you

Bulking agents for use with epoxy resins

Fumed silica	Gives a translucent fill. it may be polished to a glassy/glossy finish
Precipitated silica	As above, but will give a slightly more opaque finish
Marble dust	Good for more opaque fills, with a slightly 'gritty' texture, usually creamy coloured, good for use in reproducing Parian and other unglazed wares.
Quartz dust	As above, slightly whiter than marble dust, good for use in reproducing Parian and other unglazed wares
Talc/French chalk	Opaque, from white to grey in colour, softest of all the bulking agents, therefore is the easiest to shape and smooth
Kaolin	China clay usually produces a slightly creamy soft opaque fill.

are trying to achieve), but they are more commonly used to form an opaque white fill and then retouched to match the original.

Suitable bulking agents for all types of epoxy resin are shown in the table above.

This process as with all procedures in ceramic conservation, is one that requires patience, practice, and possibly a number of tests and trials to ensure that a suitable result is achieved. (Extensive testing before beginning work for those less experienced with the behaviour of bulking agents and colouring media is highly recommended.) However, the preliminary practice is well worthwhile because the achievement of a well-matched coloured fill will negate the need for any further retouching processes, saving valuable time.

The procedure for making a coloured fill, is as follows:

- Mix the chosen material according to manufacturers' instructions
- Divide mixture into small separate pools – one for each of the required colours
- Mix each colour separately into the small pools of resin, using either powder pigments, or epoxy colours, or a combination of the two. Ensure any powder pigments is finely ground and free of lumps before blending into the resin (see photo overleaf)
- Bulk the remaining liquid resin using a bulking agent, to match body type and translucency and/or opacity, gradually add small amounts of each coloured

Grinding and blending powder pigments into an epoxy resin

resin mixture to the larger pool to achieve desired match

- If necessary mix in more bulking agent to achieve desired consistency (usually until mixture almost begins to crumble)
- Leave for 10–15 minutes, remix and again add more bulking agent if necessary. At this stage the fill should be the consistency of a soft putty
- It can be applied to the object with suitable tools, e.g. a small spatula or the tip of a scalpel. A spatula wetted with acetone will help to smooth and shape a fill
- Allow to cure: times will vary according to the product used
  When cured, shape and abrade with scalpels/files or riflers, and suitable polishing cloths, such as Micromesh (see p.64). Be careful not to abrade/scratch any original material, any damage will be permanent
- If necessary, repeat the process to fill the gap and achieve the desired finish
- Finish the fill by polishing with a plastic polish, e.g. Greygate, see p.62
- By stretching clingfilm tightly over the final layer of an epoxy fill, it may be possible to achieve a smooth

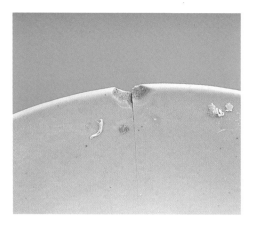

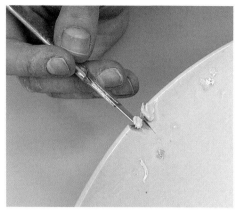

Above left: detail of gap to be filled
Above: applying coloured fill to gap

glossy finish that requires little or no further work.

Sometimes a fill can be achieved by using one layer of the mixed colour, more often it will require two or more layers perhaps with each layer having a slight colour variation. Generally subsequent layers may need to be more translucent than the underlying layers.

The colour change in the curing of the fills is usually negligible, but tests should be carried out to check before applying any material to an object.

- Where non-colour matched fill has been used, make sure that the filling is completely smooth, as any tiny blemishes will show up once a layer of paint is applied

Using a high-viscosity resin to make a fill

Measure out equal quantities of the resin, mix in enough titanium dioxide or other whitening agent (or for a coloured fill dry pigment and/or epoxy colour) to give the desired colour and then enough talc (or other bulking agent) to make a malleable putty. The more bulking agent added, the softer the putty becomes when set, and the easier it is to shape and smooth. However, the more bulking agent added, the less sticky the filler becomes, so that one must work out a happy medium. Generally, the smaller the missing chip, the stickier the filler needs to be since it has less surface area to which to adhere. To fill in a crack or chip, use the edge of a scalpel or tip of a small palette knife and press the filling in. Shape and smooth with a palette knife wetted with acetone. This same putty, heavily bulked, can be used to model up

Above: *the damage to this object was colour-filled with Fynebond epoxy resin bulked with fumed silica and tinted with manganese blue, cerulean blue, primary blue, raw umber, zinc white and chrome yellow powder pigments. When dry, the fills were abraded and polished with Micromesh*

Above right: *the filled area was then airbrushed with Rustins plastic coating, slightly tinted with powdered pigments (as above) in order to build up the glaze and replicate the colour variations on the original glaze. Each layer was polished using 6000–8000 grade Micromesh and to replicate the crazing, the tip of a pencil was used to 'draw' in the crazing. The pencil lines were rubbed very gently with a soft cloth in order to make them fainter, and a final top coating of clear Rustins was applied and once dry, was polished using Greygate plastic polish*

Right: *the finished vase*

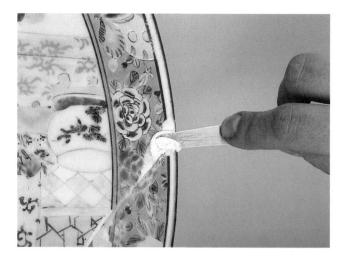

Left: Applying fill made with Araldite precision and talc to the gap

Below: pressing the fill into the gap

missing parts such as handles, arms, fingers etc. See below 'freehand modelling'. Milliput can also be used where opaque fills are required (see 'freehand modelling').

Casting with epoxy resin

These same epoxy resins (used for bonding) may also be used for casting. There are many casting resins available but for smaller casts these resins can give excellent results. Another casting resin (not previously mentioned) used for ceramic conservation is Araldite resin AY103 and Hardener HY956. Trials will have to be undertaken to find the best resin for each situation.

Different resins will give different properties in terms of finished cast, texture, translucency etc. Working times of different resins will vary, but as a general principle slower setting, low viscosity resins will tend (if used carefully) to give a cast with less air bubbles or other defects. Araldite Precision can also be used and is good for small casts. It is used in the same way as all other casting resins.

The epoxy resins should be made up according to manufacturer's instructions, and can then be whitened, and/or coloured, and bulked if and as necessary, as for fillers (see pp. 61–63). When the correct opacity and colour (and possibly texture) has been obtained, the mixture should be left to stand for five to ten minutes, and then brushed or poured very slowly into the mould.

Make sure that it flows (or is brushed) into all areas, particularly if the mould contains small sections (e.g. a mould of a small hand or foot). Tap the mould gently to allow any air bubbles to rise to the surface and prick these with a needle or cocktail stick.

> ### Notes
> - For moulds with undercuts the resin may first be brushed into the mould before pouring
> - Small moulds for intricate shapes, e.g. hands are best filled with an unbulked low viscosity resin

Araldite colours
These are liquid epoxy colours for use with epoxy resins. They are able to produce intense colours, which is very useful when replicating for example, black jasper ware or the vivid colours that are found on majolica wares. Used in extremely minute quantities they are able to produce a clear transparent mixture.

Finishing with micromesh
When shaped, the fills should be polished with micromesh cloths. Use each grade of cloth in sequence to achieve a really good finish. The final layer needs to be polished to match the glaze of the object.

The micromesh polishing system consists of precision graded silicone carbide or aluminium oxide crystals adhered onto a cushion layer with a flexible backing. These cloth-backed cushion abrasives are used for polishing rather than abrading. Micromesh is available in nine grades ranging from 1500 to 12,000 grit. It is preferable to work progressively through all the grades to achieve a completely smooth surface. By doing this a regular scratch pattern can be established and with each subsequent grade of micromesh the scratch pattern becomes more uniform. It is important to work the micromesh in one direction only and not in a circular motion. This smooth surface can be polished by the higher grades of micromesh (6,000–12,000) to the required matte/satin/gloss finish. If necessary a plastic finish polish can be used over the fill for a final high gloss translucent finish.

To be used wet, micromesh should be pre-soaked in water. Do not allow the build up of abraded particles – keep the cloths clean and wash out with soap or detergent as necessary, allow to dry and always store in a dust free environment. Micromesh is re-usable unless totally worn out.

Plaster products for fills, casts and finishing

For earthenwares or any other low-fired or unfired wares plaster-based products are preferable to epoxy resin casts and fills. There are two types of casting plaster ∞ (alpha) and ß (beta). ∞ plaster requires less water than ß plaster to achieve a pourable mix and will give a harder strength and greater reproduction of detail. ß plaster, once set, is easier to work than a plaster, and is therefore perhaps more compatible with 'soft' bodies, i.e. porous wares, and also where reproduction of detail is not as important, e.g making a flat fill on a tile.

Suitable plaster products are:

> Plaster of Paris
> Dental plaster
> Crystacal R

In addition, commercially-available plaster products such as Polyfilla can be used where a putty-like

Name	Type	Plaster to water ratio	Kg plaster: litre water
Dental Plaster	ß	100:60	1.65
Crystalcal R	∞	100:35	2.86

consistency of filler is required. For repairing blemishes and for fine surface finishing, other products such as Fine Surface Polyfilla, Modustuc or Flugger are used.

Mixing and casting with plaster

- Use clean water between a temperature range of 15-20°C (61–68°F). Plaster and water should always be weighed, and not mixed by volume because the density of plaster is variable. Refer to manufacturers' instruction for precise mixing ratios

> **Note:** *Increasing the amount of water will reduce strength, hardness, and expansion. Reducing the amount of water will increase strength but will also reduce porosity and permeability.*

Always use clean tools free from any old plaster mix. Weigh the plaster and water accurately and sift the plaster gently into the water, *never* put water into plaster. Allow the plaster to soak in the water for one to two minutes (this will remove air from the plaster) and while waiting gently tap the sides of the container. Stir gently and slowly ensuring that the plaster at the bottom of the bowl is mixed.

Skim off air bubbles or scum, which often develop on the surface of the mixture.

Gradually the mixture will begin to change consistency to become a uniform creamy, texture. This may take up to 20 minutes. Once the consistency is that of single cream the plaster is ready to pour. When filling a mould, pour the plaster onto one spot only in a steady thin continuous stream, letting the plaster flow freely. For small areas to be filled, paste in the plaster using appropriate tools.

Before the plaster has fully set, where possible, excess may be removed by scraping away with a suitable tools. Once dry, the plaster may be shaped/cut to the required profile. Scalpels, files, riflers, and sandpaper are all suitable tools. All plaster casts should be consolidated with a 5–10% solution of Paraloid B-72 in acetone. This should be applied on a soft artist's brush or applied with a plastic pipette. Where possible, for example, in the case of pieces that have been cast separately it is preferable to immerse the cast in enough consolidant to cover it completely. Leave it in the solution until no

Notes

- Do *not* attempt to remove the plaster from a cast until it has completely hardened and dried
- The physical properties of plaster will change during its lifetime, causing a change in plaster to water ratios. Plaster is hygroscopic, that is, it readily absorbs water from the atmosphere. These factors will combine to lengthen setting time and produce a reduction in set strength
- When using plaster to fill earthenware-bodied objects, make sure that any exposed body areas which are to be filled, are first consolidated with a 5 or 10% Paraloid B-72 solution. See page 48 for details of making consolidation solutions of Paraloid B-72 in acetone
- Small blemishes can be filled with a 'fine surface' finishing product such as fine surface Polyfilla, or the continental equivalent Modustuc or Flugger. This is lightly spread over the blemished area, allowed to dry, then smoothed with flour papers or Micromesh cloths. This process can be repeated as necessary

more air bubbles are seen rising (about 5–10 minutes), remove and allow to dry. The cast is now ready for retouching.

Making coloured fills with plaster

It is possible to make coloured fills with plaster. Suitable colouring media are either dry powder pigments or acrylic colours. It is difficult to achieve a dark colour using powdered pigments, and so therefore, darker coloured plaster fills/casts are more easily achieved using Golden opaque acrylic airbrush colours. See Chapter 7 on retouching for materials suitable for this method.

When using dry powder pigments, the pigments must be mixed into the dry plaster. It is suggested that if more plaster than necessary is coloured, this will allow for some initial tests. The addition of more pigments for a more intense colour or the addition of more plaster for a less intense colour may be used to adjust the colours. The same principle may also be applied to the use of acrylics, except that the acrylic colours must be added to the water, not to the dry plaster. The results of the test blocks will show if the colours need to be intensified by the addition of more acrylic paint or diluted by the addition of more water or perhaps white acrylic paint.

Notes for filling and casting
- Tests should be carried out to ensure a good colour match because the mixture will become lighter in colour as it dries. To test mix a small sample of the pre-coloured plaster with water, allow to dry and check dry sample against the object to be filled. Remember to mix a sufficient quantity of coloured plaster for all the fills of the same colour, especially if a fill cannot be completed in one go
- In any event tests will have to be carried out to determine the final shade of colour, because the application of a consolidant and any glazing media may have an effect on the plaster. The finished plaster once glazed and consolidated may look quite a different colour from both the wet and dry mix
- Use leftover plaster to make blocks for later retouching trials
- All of these products may be used without the addition of pigments, in which case they may need to be over-painted when dry to achieve a correct colour match

Using Polyfilla
Mix the plaster according to manufacturer's instruction to create a mixture thick enough to be pressed onto the area to be filled. Shape the fill with a spatula wetted with water, leave to dry and shape again with abrasive papers to achieve the correct profile. It can then be finished with flour paper or Micromesh finishing cloths (see p. 64). When this stage has been completed satisfac-

torily, the fill may then be painted and glazed if necessary (see Chapter 6).

Using Fine Surface Fillers

Fine Surface Polyfilla or Modustuc are pre-mixed plaster products that can be used to fill fine cracks and shallow gaps of less than 1–2mm (⅛in.). Flugger is an acrylic product that is used for the same purpose. These products are not suitable for filling larger areas because they have little or no adhesive properties and they also shrink slightly when set and will therefore drop out. To use, spread the product onto the required area(s) using the tip of a small spatula, allow to dry and smooth with Micromesh.

Freehand modelling

Freehand modelling is generally used where there is no existing part from which to take a cast. Sometimes objects are unsuitable for taking a mould from because the surface of the object is friable or porous, or perhaps because the shape is complicated and contains many undercuts (or cavities). Any moulding material will get caught under the undercuts and will need to be cut through in order to remove it without damage to the object. It is possible to block off these undercuts with plasticine in order to be able to remove the mould, but they will then need to be recut into the cast. This may make the process more time-consuming than freehand modelling.

Freehand modelling requires a great deal of skill, and an ability to judge size and angles. It is possible to model straight onto an object, but where the modeller is not experienced it maybe better to model the piece and attach it once finished. It is also possible to model up a piece on the bench, attach it to the object and finish it *in situ*. Once attached to the object, it is usually easier to judge size and angles etc.

For freehand modelling the simplest product to use is an epoxy putty. It can be made up as described on p.61 (using high viscosity resin to make a fill), or alternatively a ready-made putty can be purchased. The best and most useful of the epoxy putties is Milliput, a versatile product which is available in several colours. Milliput has a fairly long working life and is therefore ideally suited for fine modelling work.

The two parts, putty and hardener, are mixed together in equal quantities, and it is important to ensure that quantities are equal and that the mixing is through. While still pliable, it will attach to the break surface without adhesive.

Milliput can be shaped using a variety of implements (e.g. spatulas, cocktail sticks and scalpels) as well as water. While still pliable it should be modelled as closely as possible to the same shape as the missing part. When set, the Milliput can be further finished using scalpels, needle files and rifflers (shaped files). Final finishing with abrasive papers and then progressively finer grades of Micromesh abrasives or flour paper should create a completely smooth surface.

Note: Milliput may also be used where an opaque filler is required. It is mixed, applied to the area to be filled, shaped as much as possible while still pliable and can then be finished as described above.

Notes

- *Any retouching media applied over the top of a modelled part will remove some of the definition of that part, e.g. fingernails or fine details on hands. Remember therefore to define features more than initially seems necessary*
- *For flat shapes, modelling material may be rolled out with a rolling pin. Use talc to dust and cut to shape using a craft knife, scalpel or cake icing cutter for flower shapes*
- *Practise freehand modelling with plasticine or other re-usable modelling material before using an epoxy putty*

Moulding

This is a process whereby a missing part can be replicated and replaced using an existing detail on the piece itself or on another similar piece (for example a cup handle). An impression is taken of the extant detail and the impression material is then filled with a liquid fill (as

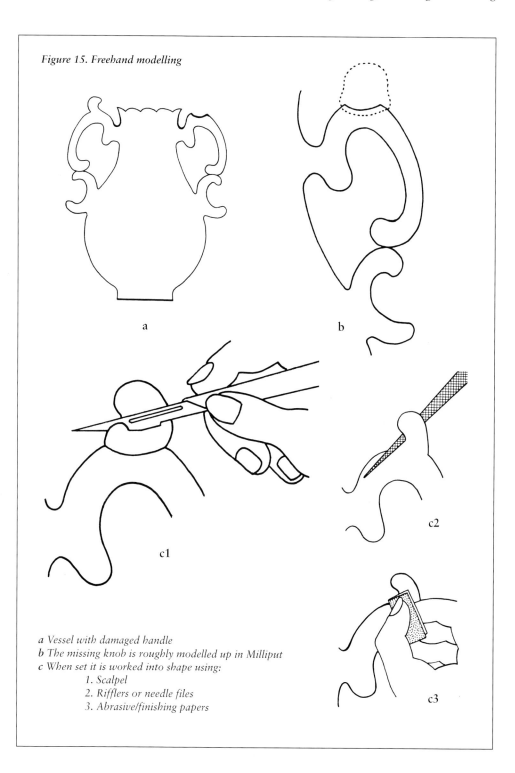

Figure 15. Freehand modelling

a

b

c1

c2

c3

a Vessel with damaged handle
b The missing knob is roughly modelled up in Milliput
c When set it is worked into shape using:
      1. Scalpel
      2. Rifflers or needle files
      3. Abrasive/finishing papers

described above) to make a cast of the required piece. When set, the cast is removed from the mould and fixed into position on the object using a suitable adhesive. This is a particularly good way of replicating complicated or difficult shapes. However, moulding materials such as silicones are expensive and the mould making is a technically challenging process, so for the one-off piece the repairer may prefer to model freehand in any event. Where no extant detail is available the missing piece will have to be modelled freehand.

Impression materials

The choice of impression material will depend on the type of mould required to cast the replacement piece. Before using any impression material, ensure it is suitable and compatible by testing if necessary on an inconspicuous area, to check that it does not stain the body or remove any surface detail. Take particular care with unglazed and low-fired wares (earthenware). Whilst silicone and other rubber compounds are useful for replicating fine detail on glazed ceramic bodies, they should be used with caution on porous earthenware because they may stain the body. If it is not possible to use any impression material because of the delicate nature of the ceramic body then the missing detail(s) will have to be made by the freehand method.

There are many impression materials available. The most commonly used ones for conservation are: dental wax, rubber latex, silicone rubber and silicone putty.

Dental wax

These pink wax sheets about 200mm x 75mm (8in. x 3in.) are very useful for simple moulds, and with some ingenuity can be applied to many projects. They are useful for achieving a correctly shaped fill on a vessel that is accessible from both the inside and outside. The wax can be softened in hot water or with a hair dryer. When soft it is pressed gently onto an existing area and allowed to harden. It can then be carefully removed, reapplied to the missing area, and filled using an appropriate filler. It is possible to use several sheets at once (soak them in hot water and press together) where a more robust mould is required, e.g. for a large area that requires extra support.

A typical use of a dental wax mould would be for the

and modelling

ject with rim chip

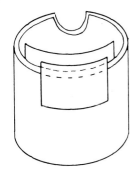

eating shaped profile on an intact edge

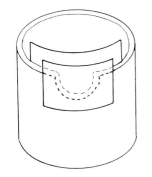

pplying the wax to the missing area

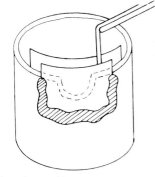

Filling the mould

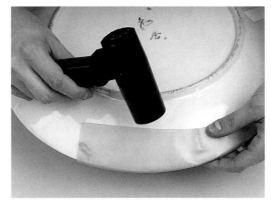

repair of a rim chip. (Wax is not suitable for larger epoxy resin fills due to the heat generated during curing.)

Before making the mould, cut the wax sheets to size, making them approximately 1.5 cm (¾ in.) wider than the gap to be filled.

The drawings here clarify the following steps:

• Soften wax and apply to both sides of an intact edge (b)

• Coat the wax sheets with a polyvinyl alcohol (PVA) release agent or a very thin coat of vaseline to prevent the wax sticking to the casting material. Add one or two drops of washing-up liquid to the bottle of release agent to help break up the surface tension

• Remove the wax moulds from the intact edge and fix and seal onto the area to be filled, using magic tape or plasticine. Be careful not to distort the mould or remove any surface decoration (c)

• Pour in liquid fill (plaster or epoxy as

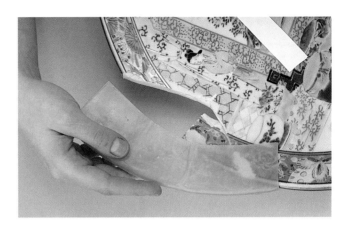

appropriate, see p. 58) making sure it runs into all the gaps of the break edge. When filled to slightly above the rim tap gently to remove air bubbles or release them by bursting with a needle or cocktail stick

• Wait until the fill is completely set before removing the wax sheets. Remove excess fill and abrade to a suitable finish

A similar technique can be used to fill in missing areas of body on vessels (e.g. plates, cups, bowls). In this case dental wax impressions should be taken of the body from the face side and the filling pressed in from the underside. The filling should be smoothed down using a spatula wetted in acetone for an epoxy fill, or with water for a plaster fill before the filler is completely hardened.

Rubber latex

Rubber latex is versatile and relatively inexpensive. It is applied in successive thin coats and left to dry for about ten minutes to half an hour at 20°C (68°F). About six coatings may be necessary before the final coat. This final coat consists of latex mixed with a bulking agent (e.g. talc or fine wood flour) and is used to support the thin latex layers. The impression is then removed (cutting and resealing if necessary) before being filled with an appropriate casting material. Copydex adhesive (rubber latex adhesive) can be used in the same way as rubber latex solution.

Silicone rubber compounds

Silicone rubber is a material that is able to reproduce minute details extremely accurately. Silicone rubbers are flexible, remain stable within a large temperature range (although temperature and relative humidity will affect setting times). They will usually peel away from non-porous surfaces without the need of a release agent, and moulds may be re-used, albeit on a limited basis. Repeated epoxy resin casts from a silicone rubber mould will cause deterioration in the silicone rubber; this will eventually result in a binding between the silicone and epoxy.

Silicone rubbers are mixed with a catalyst in order to speed up the setting time. Many different products are available, one product in common usage is Wacker silicone rubber, although preference for a product may depend on availability and cost.

When mixing silicone rubbers the amount of catalyst added is critical, so always refer to the manufacturer's instructions for mixing ratios and observe the health and safety regulations about the irritant nature of the catalyst.

If using a low viscosity silicone rubber then stir the rubber before use. Waxed paper or plastic cups are ideal for mixing the rubber. If a large quantity of rubber is required, then mix several small quantities rather than one large amount. This will ensure that the mixing is thorough and even. Allow the mixed batch to stand for a few minutes to allow air bubbles to escape.

One-part moulds

One-part moulds are more suitable for replicating

smaller details. The advantages of this type of mould are that they are a quick, relatively simple procedure, and that the resulting cast will not have any seams. Steramould, which is a silicone putty, is ideal for one-

---

Notes
- *Silicone rubber compounds are useful for replicating fine detail on glazed ceramic bodies, but they should be used with caution on porous earthenware as they may stain the body. The oil in the silicone may penetrate an unglazed/porous surface. If in doubt carry out a test in an inconspicuous area of the object first*
- *Objects should be robust enough to withstand being used for taking a mould from. The surface of the object should not be porous, or friable.*
- *All surfaces must be clean*
- *Firing cracks, chips or undercuts should be filled with plasticine, wax or other easily removable material before applying any moulding material*

---

part moulds – it is easy and quick to use and mix, and if used carefully will give excellent results. Once mixed (according to the manufacturer's instructions), it is pressed onto the detail to be replicated and left to set. This usually takes about 5–10 minutes. Once set, it should be carefully removed, checked for defects, and if it is satisfactory, it is then ready to be filled with the chosen casting material.

Sometimes it may be necessary to cut the mould in order to remove it without damaging the object. If this is necessary, use a scalpel or scissors to cut down the centre of the outside edge, and open it carefully and peel away. If the cut is made in a jagged pattern, then the edges will have a natural key and will fit together with greater accuracy. The cut mould needs to be resealed, preferably with silicone sealant or alternatively with elastic bands or superglue before pouring in any casting material.

Low viscosity silicone rubbers are also good for making one-part moulds, the preparation required is more than that required for use with a silicone putty.

Position the object on a base, a glass sheet or strong

Replicating a tile: the tile to be replicated

Building Lego walls around the tile which has previously been affixed onto a glass sheet using heavy duty double-sided sticky tape. This is to prevent the silicone rubber flowing underneath the tile

Pouring on the silicone rubber

Mould and cast of tile made in Crystal casting plaster

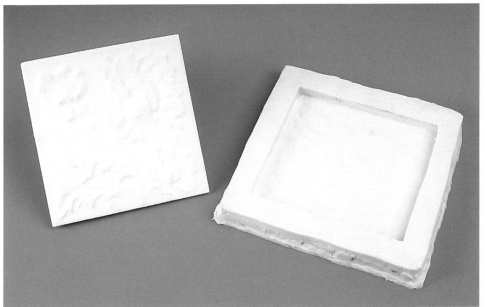

piece of card is suitable, and hold in place with double-sided sticky tape. A 'box' then needs to be constructed around the base onto the glass or card. The box can be made of Lego bricks, cardboard, wood, or other suitable material. The premixed silicone rubber is poured slowly and gently onto the object, and allowed to flow slowly into the box and over the object and into the box. This slow pouring will help to ensure that no air is trapped. Once the silicone is set, the object should be removed, and the resulting mould is then ready for use.

Making a two-piece mould

A further development of impression taking is where the mould is taken in two separate halves and then joined together. This method should be used where the shape is particularly complicated and/or contains undercuts. It is also a good way of taking an impression of a delicate area, since the risk of further damage is minimised by the separate removal of each half of the impression.

- Roll out a block of plasticine and apply over one side of the handle to be replicated, (see below)

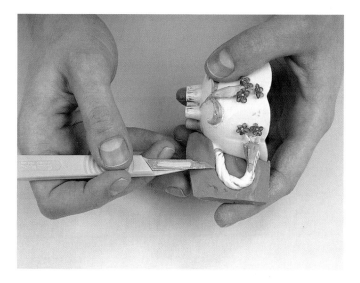

- Use a pencil to press two or three indentations into the plasticine; these will be the locating points of the two-piece mould, (see overleaf, top)

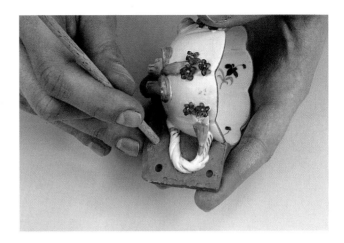

- Press the impression compound onto the side that is not covered by the plasticine barrier, (see below)

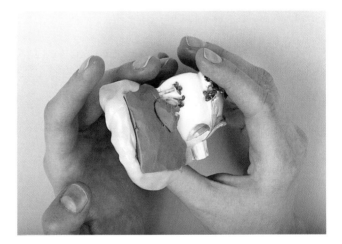

- When the impression compound has set, remove the plasticine, making sure you remove all traces from the ceramic and impression compound. Leave impression compound *in situ* (opposite, above)

- Coat the inside of the *in situ* impression material with a PVA release agent or a very smooth thin coat of Vaseline, to prevent the two parts from sticking to each other once further impression compound has

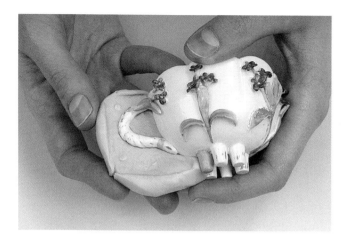

been applied to the other side of the handle

- Press more impression compound onto the exposed side of the handle (see below)

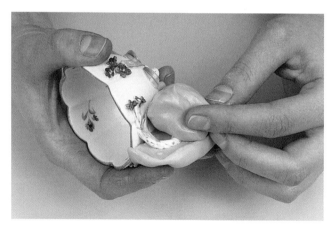

- When set, the mould should be peeled away from the object in two separate parts (above), and then these two parts closed tightly with tape, elastic bands, superglue or silicone sealant. The location dimples will assist in the re-aligning of the two parts, which must be exact

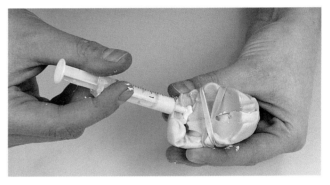

- Fill the mould with chosen casting material (above)

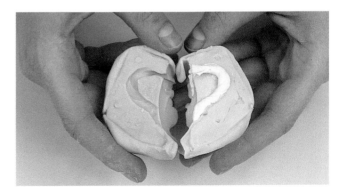

- Separate the mould and remove the cast once it has set hard (above)

- Support the mould with plasticine or on a small cork ring after pouring the casting material into the hole at the top of the handle

Note: A mould can be made in more than two parts if the shape is very intricate or large. Plasticine can be used to fill in some undercuts if this will help to make a simpler mould.

In situ casting Sometimes it is possible (and preferable) to cast missing pieces directly onto the object (see below). This often results in a more accurate cast and lessens the need to alter it in order to make it fit accurately. Another advantage of direct casting when using an epoxy resin is that it will bond itself in place. Plaster casts often need to be bonded to the object with an appropriate adhesive (solvent-based adhesive) because plaster itself has no adhesive properties.

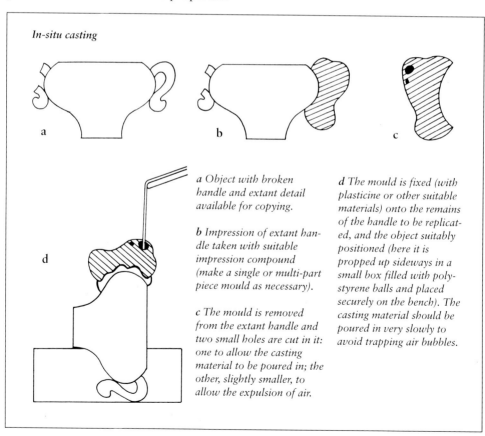

In-situ casting

a   b   c

d

a Object with broken handle and extant detail available for copying.

b Impression of extant handle taken with suitable impression compound (make a single or multi-part piece mould as necessary).

c The mould is removed from the extant handle and two small holes are cut in it: one to allow the casting material to be poured in; the other, slightly smaller, to allow the expulsion of air.

d The mould is fixed (with plasticine or other suitable materials) onto the remains of the handle to be replicated, and the object suitably positioned (here it is propped up sideways in a small box filled with polystyrene balls and placed securely on the bench). The casting material should be poured in very slowly to avoid trapping air bubbles.

Where the mould is to be cast *in situ* two holes will need to be made in the mould, one to allow the casting material in and the other to allow the escape of air. These holes should be made in the highest part of the mould. The mould should then be fixed *in situ*, using plasticine or another appropriate material (perhaps more of the same material used to take the impression). The casting material is slowly poured into one hole and the object tapped gently to allow the air bubbles to rise and escape. The casting material should be allowed to set before removing the mould, the cast should then be finished as described below.

- Where there is no extant part it is possible to model the piece up in plasticine or other appropriate modelling material. An impression is taken of the temporary mould, and once the moulding material has set, the plasticine is removed from the mould and it is ready to use

Finishing
When the liquid fill (plaster or epoxy) has fully set, remove the moulding material and carefully remove the cast. Trim, shape and abrade the cast as necessary. Any small air holes or gaps will need to be filled with the appropriate materials and then the whole area or piece finished to a smooth unblemished surface with Micromesh cloths. When this stage has been satisfactorily completed the area may then be retouched if necessary. In the case of a plaster cast, consolidate with an appropriate consolidant as described previously.

6. Retouching

When the ceramic has been rebuilt and any gaps filled, the next stage, where necessary, is colour matching for replication of surface glaze and decoration. This can take many different forms. For example, it will be fairly simple to paint on a clear coating over a well-coloured fill to simulate a clear glaze, but for other pieces it may be necessary to apply several tinted coatings, perhaps with each coat having a slight variation in colour, in order to achieve the correct depth of colour, opacity or translucency etc. There is a wide variety of different types of glazes: some may be thick and glassy, while others may be thin and translucent; sometimes the glaze may 'sit' on the clay body, while other glazes are more close fitting. Some ceramics are unglazed and matt in appearance, for example Parian and terracotta.

The retouching and colour matching of a ceramic repair is potentially the most challenging part of the repair process. There are many types of surface to simulate and a wide range of materials from which to choose, and it may be necessary to undertake many trials (and suffer many errors!) to achieve the correct colour, texture and finish.

Binding agents
A binding agent is the substance which holds the pigment in the paint. This can take many forms:

Adhesives
The low viscosity adhesives Araldite 2020, Hxtal NYL-1, and Fynebond can all be used to simulate a glaze on a repair. These adhesives may also be used as binding agents for the application of colour, either in the form of artists' dry powder pigment or Araldite colours, these resins are not compatible with acrylic paints.

Colours

Powder pigments

Pigments essentially fall into two categories: inorganic (I) which are pigments derived from nature. This type of pigment includes earth, mineral and synthetic (IS) groups; and organic pigments (O), which are based on carbon and can occur either naturally or be synthesised in which case they are known as synthetic organic pigments (SO). Inorganic pigments are insoluble, metallic compounds, which are generally dense, opaque, matt and have low tinting stength. Organic pigments on the other hand are clean, transparent, bright mixtures with a high tinting strength.

Only good quality powder pigments, which can be purchased from hobby or art shops, should be used. Because only minute amounts of pigment are needed for retouching, small quantities will last a long time. Some pigments are finely ground, while others may be coarse. All pigments should be thoroughly ground on a white ceramic tile with the tip of a spatula to get rid of any lumps before adding to the binding agent. *Dry pigments are potential irritants and care must be taken to avoid absorption either by inhalation or ingestion.*

The following is a list of some of the most commonly used colours and their properties:

Alizarin crimson (NO) vivid, highly transparent bluish deep red colour, produces rosy pink when mixed with whites.

Burnt sienna (I) earth colour, coppery-red transparent colour, adds warmth, gives salmon or peach tints when mixed with whites.

Burnt umber (I) a rich dark reddish-brown; stronger tinting abilities than raw umber and gives clear tints when mixed with whites.

Cadmium (IS) toxic-reds light or medium cadmium red for a bright red; dark cadmium red for a deeper coloured red. These reds are opaque with a strong tinting power. Mix with yellow to make orange. Will not mix with blue to produce purple.

Cadmium yellow (IS) toxic – a strong opaque colour that is obtainable in light (lemon), medium and dark (golden) with good tinting power. Mix with blue for green and mix with red for orange.

Cadmium orange (IS) toxic a bright, strong, opaque orange; more yellow than red.

Cerulean blue (IS) a bright, deep green-blue that is weak and transparent.

Cobalt blue (IS) bright, clear blue that produces cool and subdued tones; a weakish colour and tint.

Lemon yellow (IS) toxic a light, pale, opaque greenish-yellow with weak tinting power; use to make vivid oranges and greens.

Mars black (IS) darkest black – a strong colour; can be used to make tones.

Monastral blue (SO) a vivid, strong blue. It will make bright purples and greens when mixed with crimson and yellow respectively. Makes sky blue when mixed with white.

Monastral green (SO) a deep and bright colour. A very strong colour with excellent tinting ability. Can be mixed with white to make pale blue-green.

Olive green (mixture of pigments) a dull brown-green with average tinting abilities.

Raw umber (I) toxic earth colour, cool, greenish-brown; used to tone and darken other colours. Semi-transparent; has poor tinting power.

Raw sienna (I) an opaque sandy colour; fairly good tinting strength; useful for flesh tones.

Titanium white (IS) a dense opaque pigment with good tinting power – can make paler hues as well as alter a colour profoundly.

Ultramarine blue (IS) a brilliant transparent true blue; least green of the blues; mix with crimson to make purple. Mix with yellow to make greens.

Ultramarine violet (IS) a transparent deep blue-purple with good tinting power.

Yellow ochre (I) a dark, dull (earth) yellow. Semi-transparent; good tinting strength. Use with blacks and blues to give dull greens. Mix with white, burnt sienna and blue for flesh tones.

Zinc white (IS) semi-opaque white, will produce subtler tints than titanium white.

Types of retouching media

Rustins plastic coating
This is a commonly used material, which can produce excellent results. It can be coloured using finely ground

dry pigments, or used without colour as a clear coating or to replicate a glaze. It can be applied by hand, or with an airbrush. Rustins is a solvent-based product, with pungent thinners, it must be used with appropriate regard to health and safety. These include working in an area with adequate ventilation, guarding against ignition sources and high temperatures which could cause vapours to ignite. Extraction equipment, safety goggles, and protective clothing should be used.

Acrylic paint

With the recent advances that have been made in acrylic paint technology, combined with the fact that this type of paint currently carries no or minimal health-and-safety warnings, it is becoming the retouching medium of choice. Acrylic paint is pigment bound in an acrylic (plastic) binding medium. This binding medium (polymer emulsion) is milky white when wet, and dries to become clear, transparent, and glossy. Acrylics are available in a vast range of colours and textures from a variety of manufacturers, with a particularly excellent range available from Golden. Acrylics are relatively cheap and easily available.

As acrylic paint dries the water evaporates and the plastic particles join together to form a cohesive coloured film. The loss of water causes a change in the refractive index (i.e. a change in the angle of reflected light), the consequence of which is to make the paint dry to a slightly darker shade. This has to be compensated for when colour matching. The easiest way to do this is by allowing a small test sample to dry on an unrestored part of the object, or alternatively a piece of Melinex film, or ceramic tile and then checking that the dried sample is the correct colour match.

For thin films drying may take a few days, for very thick films this could be as long as weeks or more. However, for the amounts of retouching media usually used in this process, the drying time can, to all intents and purposes, be considered in hours or possibly a day or two rather than weeks. On a practical level, this fast drying will allow for the application of several thin layers within a very short space of time, depending on the environmental conditions. However, this quick drying may also prove a disadvantage in not allowing much time to manipulate the paint; in which case an extender medium may be used to retard drying time.

The Golden range of acrylics
Heavy body acrylic which is the original type of acrylic paint, and has a thick buttery consistency. Heavy bodied paint is recommended for application by hand and is particularly useful where an impasto (raised) finish is required. Each heavy body colour is formulated differently depending on the nature of the pigment. Colours that tolerate higher pigment 'loads' dry to a more opaque, matt finish. Colours that are more reactive and do not accept high pigment loading dry to a glossy finish and tend to be more transparent. Diluting heavy body colours with water usually gives disappointing and undesirable results, in terms of loss of intensity of colour and adhesion of the paint. A specialist diluter should be used if required.

Fluid acrylics have a consistency similar to heavy cream. The colours are strong although the paint is considerably thinner than the heavy bodied type. Because there are no fillers or extenders added, the pigment content is comparable to the heavy body acrylics. Diluting the heavy body acrylics with water will not produce a fluid colour consistency. Fluid acrylics may be sprayed through an airbrush or applied by hand. They may require diluting before spray application.

- to use either heavy body colours or fluid acrylics through an airbrush dilute with transparent airbrush extender
- addition of water greater than 10–15% will affect the spray and performance of the paint
- diluting with water alone will result in a mixture that will clog the airbrush, and that will probably run, and give a weak film that has poor adhesion to the substrate

Airbrush colours have been designed specifically for use in the airbrush, although they may also be used for hand retouching. Because of their low viscosity it is not necessary to dilute them. (This results in more time spraying and less time troubleshooting and cleaning the airbrush!) The colour saturation is excellent, so intense colours may be obtained without the need for multiple layers.

Transparent airbrush colours These are approximately one tenth the strength of the opaque colours, and are invaluable in reproducing tinted glazes, and generally for obtaining subtle, transparent colouring effects.

Using acrylics

Generally when mixing colours of different transparencies, the opaque colours will have greater impact on the mixture. For greater opacity mix colours with titanium white, this will give a dramatic colour change with darker colours, but for a less dramatic change in colour or opacity use zinc white. Zinc white can also be used to create subtle tints. To make colours more transparent admix with a glaze medium such as porcelain restoration glaze. Multiple layers of slightly different colour will give depth and sometimes a better colour match than single layers of the same colour.

Extender medium or acrylic glazing liquid extends the working time of the paint, allows greater flow and reduces brush stroke retention. Keep the brush well loaded with paint, a low load will create a drag effect, for fine lines and small details use a brush with a very fine point rather than a very small brush.

While gloss mediums will intensify colours, matt mediums de-intensify colours, a matt medium will lower the chroma (saturation or intensity) and inhibit the passage of light. Therefore the colour shift on drying will be less with the addition of a matt medium. Matt medium can also be used to aid the adhesion of a retouching layer. Apply a layer by hand or airbrush to the area to be retouched, allow to dry, then apply colour and/or glaze as required. Modify paint if necessary, harder less pliable paint has better adhesion to non-porous substrates, use either Golden airbrush transparent extender, or Golden GAC 200

Glaze effects can be created by the addition of a gritty pigment, rottenstone, or a bulking agent dropped onto a glaze. This can create a speckled and/or gritty effect. (Wait until the glaze is almost dry, then allow the chosen medium to 'drop' onto the glaze by tapping gently on a small brush held above the object.)

Golden Porcelain Restoration Glaze is a water-based glaze, available in matt and gloss. The different finishes can be admixed, or used sequentially, to achieve the desired sheen. It is one of the few products that has been

especially formulated for ceramic repair. Recommended application is by airbrush, but it is possible to apply it by hand. When applying multiple coats ensure that there is adequate drying between layers. Multiple layers will give a high gloss, which may be polished (once dry) to change the reflectance. The drying time will slow down as multiple layers are built up, therefore to speed drying between coats it is possible to use a hair dryer or heat-lamp. *Caution should be taken to avoid excessive heat or airflow which may damage the object or paint/glaze layers.*

Retouching by hand using Golden Fluid Acrylics

The application of several thin layers rather than one thick coating is recommended. Final curing should be achieved using a heat lamp. Once cured, use a dilute ammonia solution to remove. Porcelain restoration glaze (as with all acrylic products) may be affected by temperature and humidity, so these should be kept at a standard level. (See 'Environmental control' overleaf.)

MSA Varnish

Golden also manufacture a mineral spirit-based varnish, MSA Varnish. It is available in three finishes: gloss, which dries to a highly reflective finish; satin, which offers moderate reflection, similar to most matt varnishes; and matt which is exceptionally flat, and excellent for replicating the finish on, for example parian and biscuit. The different finishes can be admixed, or used sequentially, to achieve the desired sheen. MSA

Varnishes must be thinned before use. The amount of thinning is dependent upon the method of application. Use turpentine to dilute and clean, and note that while drying takes 3–6 hours, complete curing will take two weeks.

External factors also play an important part and consideration must be given to the temperature of the work area, which should ideally be between 18–24°C (65–75°F), and to the relative humidity which should be between 50%–75%. Make sure that any paint, objects and varnish are the same temperature.

MSA Varnish does carry a health and safety warning. Ensure that the correct precautions are in place before using. These include such measures as working in an area with adequate ventilation, guarding against ignition sources and high temperatures which could cause vapours to ignite. Extraction equipment, safety goggles, and protective clothing should be used.

> **Notes**
> - *Tools should be cleaned with soap and water immediately after use*
> - *The polymer binder is not resoluble when dry so keep brushes wet when working with acrylics, and clean immediately after use*
> - *Acrylic paint is difficult to remove from brushes, a proprietary cleaner will help to ensure that brushes are properly clean*
> - *Note that the 'same colour' acrylic paints from different ranges may well not be exactly the same shades of colour*
> - *All Golden acrylic products except MSA Varnish are admixable. For full details and instructions of Golden products visit their website www.goldenpaints.com*

Environmental control

The hardness and flexibility of an acrylic polymer are affected by changes in temperature (i.e. it is thermoplastic), therefore at higher temperatures the paint will become softer, more flexible and tacky. It may therefore be necessary to control the environment to prevent problems and to get optimum performance from the paint. Ideal temperatures should be around 20–30°C (68–86°F). Low temperatures (below 9°C or 16°F) will adversely effect the film formation. Relative humidity should be below 75%.

Brushes

The type of brush used for painting may also affect the quality of the final retouching. Sable or sable-and-synthetic-blend brushes are excellent for restoration purposes. Quality brushes that have a good spring and do not shed hairs will not make you a better painter, but they may help to give a better finish.

Different types of brushes will have different applications. The best way to learn and understand the application of each different type of artist brush is by practical application. The types and sizes of brushes needed will be dependent on the size of the area to be retouched, and also the desired effect.

Brushes should be chosen with care and properly looked after. A few of the more commonly used types of brush are:

Spotter Used for fine detail. These brushes are available in very small sizes (00000) to much larger 6, 7, 8 and 9. The 0 or 1 sizes are the most practical as they can carry more paint than the smaller sizes and therefore do not dry out as quickly. The tip on a 0 or 1 should (in theory) give you as fine a stroke as the smaller sizes.
Flat (brights) The chisel like edge is used for colour blocking and producing a good line.
Fan This gives a soft shaded effect and is also very useful for texturing and blending colour and/or glazes.
Fine Liner (rigger brush) This has a longer than normal brush head, and is excellent for painting fine lines.

Airbrushes
An airbrush is a small hand-held tool that is connected to a compressed air supply. The air supply is used to propel a stream of paint onto the object to be sprayed. The advantage of an airbrush is that it can give a smooth area with no hard edges. It is used to cover an area with an even and smooth layer(s) of paint, glaze or both, and is therefore invaluable for background

retouching, covering large areas and for painting of modelled or cast parts, particularly those parts that have not been made *in situ*. The great danger with an airbrush is that you may end up over-spraying a much larger area than is necessary, and therefore you will end up with paint in many places on the object where it should not be. Great care must be taken to mask off areas not intended to be airbrushed. Clingfilm is especially suitable for this since it produces a masking medium that will not disturb any areas underneath, especially where there may be other retouching and the cleaning off of over-spray may remove more than is desirable.

The independent double-action airbrush is the best choice for the ceramic restorer. This incorporates variable air-paint ratios as well as being able to be controlled by a finger operated trigger action. This type of airbrush allows for a range of applications, from the painting of fine lines through to covering larger areas of background. A good supplier will explain the pros and cons of each. There are many books and videos that will give guidance and instruction on the use of an airbrush.

To master the use of an airbrush is in itself a complete skill, and as with all skills it is necessary to practise and experiment. There are many books and videos that will give guidance in the form of step-by-step instruction. Most airbrush centres are very helpful and will give advice on the use and care of your airbrush. It is also a wise precaution at the time of purchase to ensure that your airbrush centre offers servicing and spares for your equipment.

To propel the paint a source of compressed air is needed, which can be in the form of an air canister or an air compressor. An air compressor with an automatic reservoir, a moisture trap and pressure-regulating valve will offer the optimum type of air supply. There are mini-compressors through to slightly larger units available, depending upon individual needs. Canisters are obviously less expensive initially, although the cost of replacing empty canisters should not be underestimated. Contact your supplier to find the air supply best suited to your needs.

Air pressure is measured in p.s.i. (pounds per square inch) or the metric equivalent kg cm^2 (kilograms per square centimetre.) The ability to regulate air pressure will allow for experimentation to achieve different paint

Using an airbrush to spray the ground colour onto the replicated tile

effects. A low pressure (around 5–7 p.s.i.) can give a stipple effect, and high pressure (around 60 p.s.i.) will give complete atomisation. The atomisation is the fineness of the particle size being sprayed. Pressure changes will also affect the paint performance; low pressure can cause the airbrush to clog, whereas high pressure will result in large areas of over-spray. The suggested air pressure for spraying Golden airbrush and fluid colours is between 25–50 p.s.i. Make sure that you clean your airbrush thoroughly after each use, however short a that time that was.

Notes
- *Keep separate brushes for separate media, i.e. do not use the same brush for acrylic paint and for example a solvent-based paint*
- *Do not mix paint with a good brush; apply colours to a tile and mix with old or cheaper brush*
- *Always clean your brush immediately after use (in suitable solvent where appropriate), then wash in soapy warm water. Brushes also need occasional conditioning, use hair conditioner: apply, rinse well and allow brush to dry*
- *Brushes must be clean and dry before storing. When storing, keep brushes upright, i.e. do not rest a brush on its hairs, and make sure stored brushes are aired*
- *Practise with each brush to determine its applications*

Useful aids

There are many materials that may help during the retouching stage. These include amongst others: tracing paper, stencils, sponges, masking tape or masking liquid, and Frisk film. Ordinary paper may be used to produce both hard and soft masks, as can, stencils, automotive masking liquid and 3M Fine line tape. They are available from either artists' supply shops or automotive supply shops.

Gilding

Replicating gilding on a ceramic repair

Gilding is the last decoration applied to fired ceramics and it should be the last when retouching a repair. With patience and care acceptable results can be accomplished, although you must be prepared to make many tests and trial runs. Gilding is a specialised process involving a separate range of materials, but mastering the techniques and methods provides a worthwhile challenge. Of all the materials available nothing can give quite the same excellent finish as real gold leaf itself.

The area to be gilded should be clean and completely smooth and free of any blemishes. In any retouching process, any surface irregularities will become more apparent when a finish is applied.

Matching the correct colour may be done by blending gold paints, gold powders or bronze powders. When using gold leaf it is not possible to blend colours and the correct match must be made from the available selection. It is however possible to modify the appearance of the colour of the leaf by adding colouring media to the size, or distressing the gilding with pumice, rottenstone, oil or acrylic paints.

Gilding materials (except gold leaf – see opposite)

Gold enamel paints These do not give a good finished appearance and are not recommended.

Acrylic gold paint With the improvements in acrylic gold paints, these are definitely one option worth considering. Acrylic gold can be utilised in the same way as any other acrylic paint, although they may need several layers in order to achieve a depth of colour. Different makes will give different results, but as with other acrylic media Golden produce an excellent range, notably the Fluid Iridescent colours. Apply using a brush or airbrush.

Gold ink This consists of metallic particles suspended in a shellac medium. It can give acceptable results but usually needs more than one coat and lacks the lustre of real gold. Apply using a brush or airbrush.

Gold pens These are fairly good for retouching small areas although they often tend to develop a greyish tinge when dry. They may be applied directly from the pen if the nib is fine enough, or by pressing the nib several times onto a white ceramic tile. This will give you a small pool of liquid which can then be applied with a suitable brush.

Gold paint and varnishes These are metal powders suspended in a liquid medium; they are easy to apply by hand with a brush or with an airbrush. They sometimes give an acceptable finish but again these lack the lustre of real gold.

Bronze powders are available in a variety of colours, ranging from pale gold to deep copper. They can give an acceptable finish, and it is also possible to colour match by admixing different shades. Only the finest quality, non-tarnishing, burnishing bronze powders should be used. 'Burnishing' refers to the particle size of the bronze power, and not its ability to be polished. It is possible to finish bronze powder with a layer(s) of varnish, to prevent or retard any tarnishing, although this may end up giving a dulled effect to the gilded area.

Gold powder Unlike leaf gold this can be matched, but unlike bronze powders it does not tarnish. It can be blended into the original better than gold leaf can. Colour is determined by the purity of gold, which is measured in carats. The biggest drawback with gold powder is the high price. However, for the small quantities used it is worthwhile considering the investment. Excess gold powder can be returned to the container and re-used.

Using bronze and gold powders
Match the colour to the original as closely as possible, with the addition of powder pigments if necessary to obtain an exact match. Pigment must be thoroughly ground so that the resulting mixture is not lumpy. When the correct colour and texture has been obtained it can then be mixed into a binding medium (e.g. Rustins) and

applied with a hand-held brush. For application by air-brush it may be necessary to dilute the mixture with the appropriate thinning agent. Gold and bronze powders mixed with any medium must be stirred frequently during application, since heavy gold and bronze particles tend to sink to the bottom of a suspension.

An alternative and better method of applying powders is to dust the entire area with a little talc applied on a no. 7 squirrel-hair brush. The area to be gilded is then 'painted in' using a gold size (see below) or an appropriate medium mixed with a little suitable pigment, e.g. alizarin crimson for a reddish gold and mid-chrome yellow for a yellow gold. By using a tinted size it is easier to see the actual area that has been painted. When the size is tacky the powders can be applied by gently sprinkling the powder from a soft brush over the area to be gilded. When dry, brush the excess powder off, and if necessary seal using a varnish applied with an airbrush although this is not recommended.

Dutch metal (Schlag)

This is a metal leaf available in several colours in loose-leaf form. It is cheaper than Gold leaf and because it is much thicker, it is easier to handle. It is applied in the same way as gold leaf, and can initially give good visual results, but it will tarnish in time. The application of a glaze medium over the metal leaf will prevent tarnishing, but it will also cause a dulling of the leaf.

Gold leaf

Gold leaf is without a doubt the best way of restoring gilding onto ceramics. It is the only medium that can replicate the original finish, and despite the initial cost and difficulty of handling, it cannot be bettered. With practice and care it should be possible to master the techniques and materials involved. Loose gold leaf and transfer gold leaf are available in books of twenty-five leaves, the only difference being that the transfer variety is backed with a sheet of tissue paper which is peeled off when the gold is transferred. Since gold leaf cannot be blended to obtain colours it must be matched correctly before application. Colour is determined by the purity of gold, and charts for matching are available from gilding suppliers. It is possible to appear to alter the 'colour' of gold leaf, by either using a size that has been coloured by the addition of a colouring medium that is compatible with the size (e.g. powder pigment for oil size and acrylic for a water-based size), or by using two (or more) layers of different coloured leaf, and/or also by using a small amount of dry pigment or oil or acrylic paint over the top of the dried gilded area.

Gold size
Both transfer and loose gold leaf need a medium to fix them onto the ceramic. This medium is known as gold size, and is available with various drying times; the Japan variety is the quickest drying size, with a tack time of approximately twenty minutes depending on the temperature and humidity of the working environment. Other available sizes have varying tack times of between two and twenty-four hours. The slower drying sizes give better results due to the self-levelling properties being given longer to work. The longer the size takes to become tacky the better the gloss and the longer the working time you have available. Lack of working time is not, however, usually a problem when gilding onto ceramics because the working areas are generally fairly small. Also, when using a slower drying size the difficulty of keeping the object in a dust-free environment, combined with the difficulty of arranging working times, often outweighs the advantages.

Equipment
Working with gold leaf is a very delicate business and requires the following specialist equipment:

A *gilder's cushion* which is a padded, leather-covered board with a draught screen fitted around one end.
A *gilder's knife* which is used to cut the gold on the cushion, alternatively a butter knife with a straight, smooth blade can be used, which should cut the gold cleanly without damaging the cushion. Any slight nick in the blade will tear rather than cut the gold.
A *gilder's tip* Tips are brushes that are made by sandwiching a thin layer of badger hair between two pieces of card. They are available in different lengths. Generally for ceramic repairs the shortest length tip is the most useful. Tips can be cut into narrow lengths although it may be easier for an inexperienced user to use a good quality sable artist's brush, rather than a

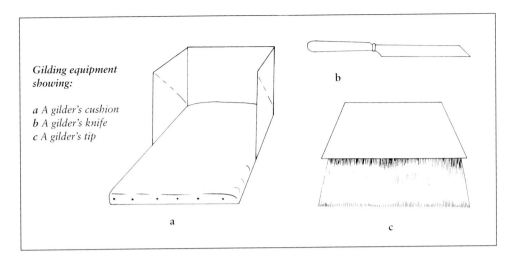

Gilding equipment showing:

a A gilder's cushion
b A gilder's knife
c A gilder's tip

gilder's tip. Smaller tips (length and width) make it easier to handle the small quantities of gold leaf. Tips should be stored so that the hairs do not become bent. It is a good idea to store them between two pieces of stiff card.

A selection of good quality sable or squirrel brushes will also be needed.

Applying gold leaf
Gold leaf is not as easy to use as the other gilding materials described in this section but with practice and care the techniques can be mastered.
1. If necessary an inexperienced gilder may find it easier to mask surrounding areas but beware of applying adhesive tape to gilded/restored surfaces; clingfilm is a better solution.
2. Before applying the size, lightly dust the area with talc, which prevents gold adhering to the surrounding area.
3. Apply size with a sable brush to the object, and at the same time several samples to a tile and wait for it to dry to a 'tacky' consistency. Use the tile to test for onset of tack (also for testing and practising) this will ensure that work is not ruined.
4. To apply loose gold, cut it on a gilder's cushion into suitable sections with a gilder's knife, lift with a gilder's tip or artists brush and lay it on the sized area. If you can do this without the gold dropping off the tip, or a

draught of air whisking it off, you are doing well!

5. When using transfer gold, the design required can be traced gently onto the back of the tissue with a soft pencil or using carbon paper; cut to the appropriate shape and apply to the sized area. The transfer leaf can be gently rubbed with a small cotton wool pad to help it adhere. Use 100% cotton wool – viscose can scratch the gold. Dust off any excess leaf with a soft artist's brush.

- blend hard edges with pumice powder, rottenstone or a 12000 Micromesh. This will only work if the gold size is completely dry. Test it first on your tile to avoid spoiling your work
- pumice powder or rottenstone can also be used to distress, and/or matt gilding
- powder pigments can be rubbed on top of the gilding to tone and give a redder/greener etc. effect
- it is also possible to use oil paint or acrylic transparent airbrush colours to tone and colour gilding
- any mistakes are better rectified once the size has dried
- cut back untidy edges and rectify mistakes with a sharpened wooden cocktail stick

Water gilding

Water gilding is gilding using water as a size. A small amount of gelatine is dissolved in warm water (approximately 0.1gm to 150ml of water) in order to give the water slight adhesive properties, and also to help reduce the surface tension of the water. It is preferable to use gelatine that is formulated for gilding, and not the sort available in a supermarket that is used for cooking. Because the gold is 'floated' on top of the water size it is only possible to use loose-leaf gold. The area is painted with the water size, and the gold leaf applied. It is then allowed some time to dry after which it should be 'waved' over a source of steam for about five seconds to set the gold. Water gilding will give a very bright and shiny appearance.

Silvered gilding

This is metal leaf usually in the form of palladium, platinum, or other precious metals, which is available in both loose and transfer leaf. It is made from non-tarnishing metals and therefore it is treated in exactly the same manner as gold leaf.

Lustres

A metallic finish or iridescent surface decoration on a ceramic body is known as 'lustre'. Until recently, a lustre finish was perhaps the most difficult finish to replicate successfully, but, with the introduction of Golden fluid iridescent paints the retouching of these areas is no longer as challenging as it once was! However, as with all other techniques described in this book, it will still need experimentation to get a good end result. When preparing an area on an object to be coated in a lustre, take the restored area back to a slightly lower level than the surrounding body in order to allow for the several coats necessary for a satisfactory combination of colour, tone and iridescence.

Techniques for simulating lustreware

The first coat over an untinted fill should match the ground colour of the object. The metallic effect can be replicated by using lustre powders (e.g. Pearlescent, Hi-lite, Glimmer), bronze or metal powders. These should be mixed into a suitable binding agent such as MSA Varnish or Rustins plastic coating, and applied by hand or airbrush. Stir the mixture frequently; metallic particles are heavy and will sink to the bottom of a suspension. The area surrounding the fill may be masked off with clingfilm if required.

Copper and bronze lustre
A dark bronze lustre finish can be achieved by adding burnt umber and indian red (mars red) powder pigment to a suitable binding medium. Apply two to three coats, then mix dark bronze powder into the same mixture and apply on top of the previously applied paint. Where necessary polish the final layers of varnish with 8000–12,000 Micromesh cloths. Other metallic finishes can be replicated in the same way as described above using the appropriate ground colours and metallic powders. A white ceramic tile is a good surface on which to practise.

Purple and pink (Sunderland) lustre
Alizarin red and ultramarine blue will give a ground

colour. The lustrous quality can be produced by adding powders from one or more of the 'hi-light' ranges, violet, pink or red as necessary.

Generally only one coat of pink lustre need be applied. Mix on a tile and practise a few brush strokes to achieve the desired effect. A sponged effect can be copied by using small pieces of natural sponge and dipping them into the premixed palette. Only when satisfied that the finish is the one which you require should you apply to the repair.

Acrylic lustres
The recreation in acrylic of lustre glazes can be achieved by varying the admixed colours. Laying these colours down on a metallic ground will add to the lustrous effect. Acrylic colours laid on a 'rough' silver ground using aluminium powder will give a good final effect even when replicating bronze lustres. Aluminium power is roughly textured and gritty, the uneven reflectance of light from such as base will contribute to, and enhance the lustre effect.

The Golden Acrylics used to replicate a Sunderland lustre are:

iridescent pearl fine
napthol red medium
quinacridone crimson
dioxazine purple

The Golden Acrylics used to replicate a copper lustre are:

iridescent copper light fine
iridescent copper fine
bright orange
raw umber

Both of the above lustres were achieved by admixing the prescribed colours and airbrushing them onto a ground of aluminium powder. The aluminium powder had been laid down using Japan gold size. The number of layers of colour required will depend on the depth of colour needed. As always it is a good idea to test onto a tile first. The abrading of the individual layers of either acrylic lustre paint (with Micromesh or any other soft

This area has been previously
filled with pollyfilla. It was then
consolidated with a 5% solution
of Paraloid B-72 in Acetone,
after which the details were
repainted by hand using Golden
Acrylic colours. The gilding was
retouched using 22ct transfer
leaf applied over Japan size

Airbrushing a previously rebonded and filled area to check
for any defects (small holes or
unfilled areas). This coat was
smoothed down using micromesh grades 4000–6000 before
finishing

abrasives is not recommended) because it will dull the lustre effect. For a smooth (to the touch) finish it is necessary to apply several layers of gloss medium, such as MSA varnish or Porcelain Restoration glaze. These can be polished to the required finish.

7. Case studies

Case study 1. of a Staffordshire figurine

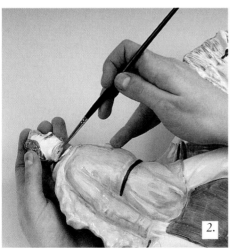

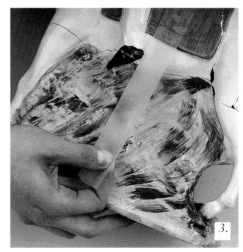

Treatment record

name of client	
description of object	Staffordshire figure of Victor Emmanuel ll circa 1860
conservation report treatment plan	Broken into 7 pieces with a large piece of the horse's hindquarters missing. An attempt has been made to rebond the shards using superglue

Treatments

debonding and cleaning	Debonding tests showed all standard solvents to be ineffective, including Nitromors, which was too viscous to penetrate the cracks. Therefore, it was decided to use pure dichlormethane. Cotton swabs were applied to the break edges and dichloromethane was applied to the swabs. The object was wrapped in cling film and then checked at regular intervals, more dichlormethane was applied as necessary. After 2-3 hours the superglue had broken down and it was possible to very gently dismantle the shards. The break edges were steam cleaned, and any further remaining adhesive was mechanically removed; the break edges were checked under a binocular microscope in order to ensure that there was no adhesive residue left, (see illustration 1 opposite).
consolidation	All break edges were consolidated using a 5% solution of Paraloid B-72 in acetone, (see illustration 2 opposite).
rebonding	50% solution of Paraloid B-72 in acetone was used to rebond the object. The shards were held in place by magic tape until the adhesive had dried, (see illustration 3 opposite).
gap fill	Polyfilla plaster was mixed to a dough-like consistency and applied to the gap in the horse's hindquarters; dental wax was used to support the fill. Once the plaster had set hard the wax was removed and the fill was shaped and abraded until it was smooth. Smaller gaps were also filled using polyfilla, finishing with a layer(s) of fine surface polyfilla where required, this was then gently abraded and polished until smooth using micromesh.
retouching	The ground colour on the horse was airbrushed using an admixture of Golden airbrush colours and fluid colours (titan buff, zinc white, raw umber and yellow oxide). Several coats were applied and when each coat was dry it was polished using Micromesh 6000-8000

A layer of Golden porcelain restoration glaze was applied and allowed to thoroughly dry. A pencil was used over the top of the glaze to fill in the crazing and this was sealed with a final coat of porcelain restoration glaze, which was polished down with an 8000 Micromesh.

All other retouching details were carried out by hand using Golden heavy body colour and finished with a coat of porcelain restoration glaze. |

Case study 2. of a Derby candle sconce

The replication of a Derby candle sconce

The original sconce was cleaned and wiped dry. A plasticine bed was built up into which the sconce was embedded using a good quality modelling plasticine. Further plasticine pieces were applied until half of the sconce including half of the inside had been embedded with plasticine.

The plasticine was butted up to the edges of the object to stop any silicone rubber flowing underneath the object, all plasticine surfaces were smoothed and levelled.

A wire turning tool was used to cut a canal in the plasticine – about 3–4mm ($^3/_8$in.) from the edge. This canal acted as a location key to ensure that the pieces of the mould would fit together exactly.

Two straws with large diameters, which were in contact with the object, were embedded in the plasticine at the top of the mould. When the straws and plasticine were removed, two channels remained in the silicone rubber cast: one channel for the casting material to be poured into the mould, and the other channel to allow the escape of air.

The plasticine embedded sconce was positioned on a small glass sheet which had been covered with heavy duty double sided sticky tape; this was used as a base for the Lego brick box (see p.78). A low viscosity, thin, silicone rubber was gently poured into the box over the object and allowed to flow until the surface of the object had been covered by a thin layer of silicone.

The silicone was then left to cure. (The time taken to cure is dependent on the type of rubber used, but it is generally advisable to leave 24 hours before applying further layers of silicone.)

Once the initial layer of silicone had cured, another layer of silicone was poured over the first layer, covering the object completely.

Once the second layer had cured, the retaining walls and modelling plasticine were removed. All traces of the plasticine were thoroughly removed from the object and silicone to ensure that the next application of silicone would not contain any impression of any residue plasticine. Removal of plasticine was undertaken very carefully to ensure that it would not disturb the mould. Any further remaining residue was removed with white spirit on a cotton swab.

The object was **not** removed from the silicone, but all the exposed areas of the silicone rubber were painted with a thin layer of release agent. The release agent was carefully painted on with a fine brush and was not allowed to touch the object.

The completed mould and cast

Retouching the cast sconce

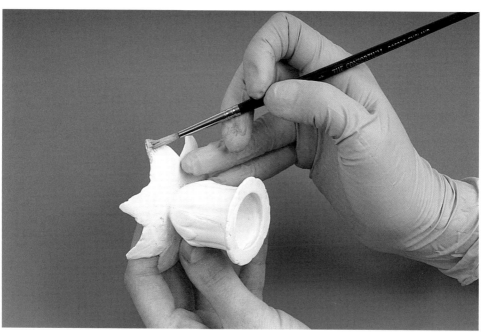

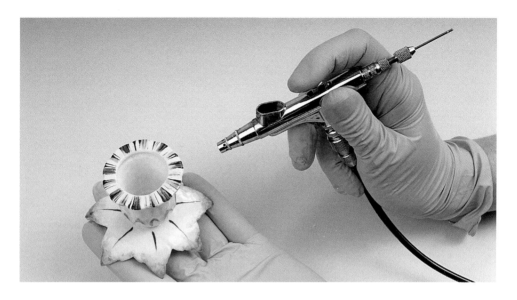

Applying the final coat of air-brushed MSA gloss varnish to the replicated sconce

The retaining Lego walls were again placed around the mould, high enough to allow the object to be totally covered by the silicone.

Two further layers of silicone were poured over the exposed area. As before the first layer was allowed to flow over the object and surrounding area and once set, a further layer was applied. When the second layer had cured the mould was opened and the object was removed.

The mould was fixed together using silicone sealant, and the casting material, Crystalcal R, was poured in through one of the channels. This was allowed 24 hours to set and was then removed from the mould. Several casts were made in order have spare samples and to use for testing retouching materials.

The best cast was chosen and the small pinholes in the plaster were filled with fine surface Polyfilla. The seam lines and any other irregular areas were abraded using 1500–3200 Micromesh. The cast was then left to soak in a 10% solution of Paraloid B-72 in Acetone. When the air bubbles had stopped rising to the surface the cast was removed and allowed to dry.

The base colour was airbrushed onto the sconce using Golden airbrush colours and details were hand painted using Golden fluid and heavy body colours.

Several final coatings of MSA Varnish were applied and polished using a 6000–12000 Micromesh where necessary.

Appendix

Glossary of terms and materials

The following list contains some of the most common materials used in ceramic repair and mentioned in this book. Equivalent American product names are given in square brackets where appropriate.

Some of these products are hazardous to health and the environment. The hazard warnings on the products indicate the degree of danger, but it is essential to read the full manufacturer's instructions regarding use, storage and disposal before use. If instructed not to breathe fumes, ensure that the room is well ventilated or use an extraction hood; in the case of dust or particles, wear a dust mask. Wear disposable gloves (or household rubber gloves for the less powerful products such as detergents) if instructed to avoid skin contact.

Acetone (Propanone) A highly flammable, irritant solvent with many uses and applications in ceramic restoration

Ammonia solution A pungent smelling solution made by dissolving ammonia gas in water. It can cause burns and is irritating to skin, eyes and respiratory system. Pressure may develop in the bottle – open with care. To use, add a few drops to hydrogen peroxide solution when removing stains from high-fired wares. Also used well diluted to remove cured Golden Porcelain Restoration Glaze

Araldite 2020 Low viscosity, slow setting, epoxy resin adhesive

Araldite Rapid High viscosity, fast setting, epoxy resin adhesive

Araldite Precision High viscosity, slow setting, epoxy resin adhesive

Barytes (barium sulphate) Used as a bulking agent

Hazard symbols

 Toxic substances which present a serious risk of acute or chronic poisoning, by inhalation, ingestion or skin absorbtion

 Harmful substances which present moderate risk to health by inhalation, ingestion or skin absorption

 Flammable extremely flammable liquids have a flash point of less than 0° and a boiling point less than or equal to 35°C

Highly flammable liquids include:
1. Those which may become hot and finally catch fire in contact with air at ambient temperature without application of energy.
2. Those which may readily catch fire after brief contact with a source of ignition and which continue to burn or to be consumed after removal of the source of ignition.
3. Those which are gaseous and flammable in air at normal pressure.
4. Those in contact with water or damp air which evolve highly flammable gases in dangerous quantities.
5. Liquids which have a flash point below 21°C

Highly flammable liquids are those having a flash point equal to or greater than 21°C and less than or equal to 55°C

 Oxidising substances which give rise to highly endothermic reactions in contact with other substances particularly flammable substances

 Corrosive substances which destroy living tissue

 Irritant substances which are non-corrosive but are liable to cause inflammation through immediate prolonged or repeated contact with the skin or mucous membranes

Biotex A proprietary brand of biological washing powder containing certain enzymes which catalyse the breakdown of proteins. Useful as a stain remover. Use one tablespoon to a litre (2 pt) of water

Calgon (sodium hexametaphosphate) A proprietary water softener used in conjunction with biological detergent to remove stains from porcelains. Use one tablespoon to a litre (2 pt) of water. Lustres and gilding may be affected

Cellulose nitrate A high viscosity solution adhesive commonly used on porous ceramics, dilute with acetone. Common brand name is HMG

Consolidate reinforce or strengthen

Crystacal R hard alpha plaster, used for casting where a hard set strength and reproduction of detail is required

Crystalline A solid with a regular and repeating geometric shape

Cyanoacrylate *see* superglue

De-ionised water Water that has been passed through a de-ionizer unit, which removes unwanted impurities (in the form of ions)

Dental plaster softer beta plaster, use on porous wares and also where reproduction of detail is not important

Dichloromethane *see* Nitromors

Distilled water Produced from the steam of boiled and condensed water

Earthenware Opaque, porous non-vitreous soft-fired ware

Emulsion A mixture of tiny particles of one liquid dispersed in another liquid

Epoxy resin Synthetic thermosetting resin

Friable Easily crumbled

Fumed silica Very finely powdered silica used as a matting agent in paints and varnishes. Also as a bulking agent for epoxy resin fills

Fynebond Low viscosity, slow setting, epoxy resin adhesive

Greygate Plastic Polish used for a final polish for epoxy resin fills. Apply, leave to dry and rub off with soft cloth

Hydrogen peroxide (H_2O_2) À bleaching agent (and disinfectant). Gives off oxygen so do not store with flammable solvents (because of fire risk). Available in volume strengths, apply onto cotton wool swabs over discoloured cracks, activate with a few drops of ammonia solution

Hygroscopic Tending to absorb water from the atmosphere

Hxtal NYL-1 Low viscosity, very slow setting, epoxy resin

Jenolite A phosphoric acid based rust remover. Use sparingly to remove iron staining from ceramics; can react with iron compounds in low fired ceramics

Kaolin China clay, hydrated aluminum silicate. Used in porcelain production: used as a bulking agent with epoxy resins

Laponite A synthetic inorganic colloid powder, which forms a thick gel when mixed with water; use as a poultice to remove ingrained stains. May be mixed with some solvents, e.g. white spirit or cleaning agents (hydrogen peroxide)

Marble powder Finely powdered marble available in different 'grit' sizes, used as a bulking agent with epoxy resins for fills on porcelain, especially Parian

Melinex [Mylar] Transparent polyester film useful as a masking film, for mixing adhesives and retouching media

Micromesh Cloth backed sanding/polishing cloth, made by adhering silicone carbide and aluminium oxide crystals onto a cloth backing

Milliput A two-part epoxy putty. Use equal amounts and mix thoroughly. Use as a filler and modelling material, sets hard in 24 hours

Nitromors [Zylonyte] (dichloromethane and methanol) A powerful degreaser, paint remover and epoxy adhesive softener; available as water-soluble (green label) or spirit soluble (yellow label). Water-soluble is preferable for ceramic restoration use. This is potentially the most hazardous material used in ceramic repair and should be used in a well ventilated area, preferably in a fume hood or with air extraction

Non-ionic detergent A detergent which produces electrically neutral colloidal particles in solution

Paraloid B-72 Co-polymer of methyl acrylate and ethyl methacrylate. A conservation 'approved' adhesive, available as granules as well as tubes. Use, for consolidation and bonding porous wares

Plaster products (hydrated calcium sulphate) Used for filling and casting

Polymer Substance which consists of many monomers (small molecules) bonded together in a repeating sequence

Relative humidity Ratio of actual vapour pressure of water in the air to that in air saturated with water vapour usually expressed as a percentage

Rubber latex A vulcanised natural rubber impression material (contains ammonia which may react with metals especially copper). Shrinks quickly; remove once set

Rustins Plastic Coating – a mixture of butylated urea formaldehyde, melamine and alkyd resins in a solvent of aromatic hydrocarbons and alcohols. The hardener is a mixture of inorganic acid and alcohol. Used for retouching and/or glazing

Silicone carbide Very hard clear crystalline compound of silicone and carbon. Mechanically strong and having fracture characteristics that make them extremely useful in abrasive papers

Silicone rubber Used as a moulding material, valued for chemical stability and wide temperature range over which they retain resiliency. Will stain porous earthenware

Steramould Silicone putty used as moulding material – may stain unglazed and/or porous bodies

Superglue A popular name for cyanoacrylate adhesives. Generally unsuitable for ceramic restoration purposes, although it may be useful for tacking shards together before 'dry sticking'. Difficult to break down; superglue remover (acetone or Nitromors) may be used. Use with caution only on high-fired wares if absolutely necessary.

Talc (magnesium sulphate) Sometimes called French chalk, a useful bulking agent for epoxy fills

Titanium dioxide An opaque, brilliant white pigment for tinting, painting and bulking epoxy resin fills

Thermosetting a material which when fully cured will not return to its original plastic state (non-reversible reaction)

Viscosity Viscosity characterises a fluid's resistance to flow

Zinc oxide A commonly used white pigment for painting, bulking and tinting. Not as intensely white as titanium dioxide

Manufacturers and suppliers in the UK

Many of the materials recommended in this book can be purchased from general DIY or hardware stores or good artists' supply shops. There are also a number of general craft suppliers which stock a wide range of restoration materials, as well as specialist suppliers of specific products. Where materials cannot be purchased directly, ask the manufacturer for details of your nearest stockist.

Araldites

(call for your nearest Vantico Authorised distributor)
Vantico Ltd
(Ciba Specialty Chemicals PLC)
Performance polymers
Duxford
Cambridge CB2 4QA
Tel: +44 (0)1223 832121
Fax: +44 (0)1223 493014 (sales)

Art/conservation suppliers

Lesley Acton Associates
10 Bow Industrial Park
Carpenters Road
London E15 2DZ
Tel: +44 (0)20 8936 1111
Fax: +44 (0)20 8936 1122
www.onlineconservation.co.uk

Stuart R Stevenson
68 Clerkenwell Road
London EC1M 5QA
Tel: +44 (0)20 7253 1693
Fax: +44 (0)20 7490 0451

Brushes and airbrushes

Artists' supply shops or

Airbrush & Spray Centre
39 Littlehampton Road
Worthing
West Sussex BN13 1QJ
Tel: +44 (0)1903 266991
Fax: +44 (0)1903 830045
www.airbrushes.co.uk
email: sales@airbrushes.co.uk

CLE Design Ltd (also lighting and air extraction equipment)
69–71 Haydens Road
Wimbledon
London SW19 1HQ
Tel: +44 (0)20 8540 5772
Fax: +44 (0)20 8543 4055
www.cledesign.com
email: john@cledesign.com

Dental Supplies

Milliput
The Milliput Company
Unit 8
The Marian
Dolgellau
Gwynedd LL40 1UU
Tel/Fax: +44 (0)1341 422562
www.milliput.com
email: info@milliput.demon.co.uk

Zahn Laboratory (A Henry Schein Company)
Medcare House
Centurion Close
Gillingham Business Park, Gillingham
Kent ME8 0SB
Tel: +44 (0) 8700 102047
Fax: +44 (0)8700 102087
www.henryschein.co.uk
email: zahnlab@herryschein.co.uk

Fynebond

Fyne Conservation Services
Airds Cottages
St Catherine's
By Loch Fyne
Argyll PA25 8BA
Tel/Fax: +44 (0)1369 860415
email:
bmckenna@directofficesolutions.fsnet.co.uk

General conservation and art specialists

Conservation Resources Ltd (UK)
Units 1, 2, 4 & 5 Pony Road
Horspath Industrial Estate
Cowley
Oxford OX4 2RD
Tel: +44 (0)1865 747755
Fax: +44 (0)1865 747035

Preservation Equipment Ltd.
Vinces Road
Diss
Norfolk IP22 4HQ
Tel: +44 (0)1379 647400
www.preservationequipment.com
email: sales@preservationequipment.com

Gilding materials

The Gilders Warehouse Ltd
5 & 4d Woodside Commercial Estate
Thornwood
Epping
Essex CM16 6LJ
Tel: +44 (0)1992 570453
Fax: +44 (0)1992 561320
www.gilders-warehouse.co.uk
email: alias@gilders-warehouse.co.uk

W Habberley Meadows Ltd
5 Saxon Way
Chelmsley Wood
Birmingham B37 5AY
Tel: +44 (0)121 770 0103
Fax: +44 (0)121 770 6512
www.habberleymeadows.co.uk
email: gold@habberleymeadows.co.uk

Laboratory suppliers

Cole-Parmer Instrument Company Ltd
Unit 3
River Brent Business Park
Trumpers Way
Hanwell
London W7 2QA
Tel: +44 (0)20 8574 7556
Fax: +44 (0)20 8574 7543
Sales freephone 0500 345 300
www.coleparmer.co.uk
email: sales@coleparmer.co.uk

Griffin & George
Bishop Meadow Road
Loughborough
Leicestershire LE11 5RG
Tel: +44 (0)1509 233344
Fax: +44 (0)1509 231893
www.griffinandgeorge.co.uk
email: griffin@fisher.co.uk

P Merck Ltd
Hunter Boulevard
Magna Park
Lutterworth
Leicestershire LE17 9XN
Tel: +44 (0)1455 558 600
Fax: +44 (0)1455 558 586
www.merckeurolab.ltd.uk
email: sales@merckerurolab.ltd.uk

R & L Slaughter Ltd (BDH)
Units 11 & 12
Upminster Trading Parks
Warley Street
Upminster
Essex RM14 3PJ
Tel: +44 (0)1708 227140
Fax: +44 (0)1708 228728
www.slaughter.co.uk
email: sales@slaughter.co.uk

Micromesh

D.E.P. Fabrications Ltd
Unit 33, Cam Centre
Wilbury Way, Hitchin
Herts SG4 0TW
Tel: +44 (0) 1462 441414
Fax: +44 (0) 1462 442110

Paraloid B-72, cellulose nitrate

HMG Paints Ltd
Riverside Works
Collyhurst Road
Manchester M40 7RU
Tel: +44 (0)161 205 7631
Fax: +44 (0)161 205 4829
www.hmgpaints.com
email: sales@hmgpaints.com

Pigments and general art supplies

A P Fitzpatrick Fine Art Materials
142 Cambridge Heath Road

London E1 5QJ
Tel: +44 (0)20 7790 0884
Fax: +44 (0)20 7790 0885
email: apscolour@aol.com

L. Cornelissen & Son Ltd
105 Great Russell Street
London WC1B 3RY
Tel: +44 (0)20 7636 1045
Fax: +44 (0)20 7636 3655
email: info@cornelissen.com

Silicone Rubbers

Ambersil (silicones)
Ambersil
Castlefield Ind. Est.
Wylds Road
Bridgwater
Somerset TA6 4DD
Tel: +44 (0)1278 424200
Fax: +44 (0)1278 425 644
www.amberchemical.com
email: mail@ambersil.co.uk

Small scales and instruments

Sentinel Laboratories Hcl
Unit 12–13
Lin D Field
Enterprise Park
Lewes Road
Linfield
West Sussex RH16 2LH
Tel: +44 (0)1444 484044
Fax: +44 (0)1444 484045
email: sendlab@globalnet.co.uk

Photographic Scales etc. (John Price)
PO Box 46
Farnham
Surrey GU9 7XE
Tel: 01252 721455
email: arc.con@btinternet.com

Specialist Books

Archetype Books
6 Fitzroy Square
London W1T 5HJ
Tel: +44 (0)20 7380 0800
Fax: +44 (0)20 7380 0500

Reference Works
12 Commercial Road
Swanage
Dorset BH19 1DF
Tel: +44 (0)1929 424423
Fax: +44 (0)1929 422597
www.referenceworks.co.uk
email: sales@referenceworks.co.uk

Steramould

A & M Hearing Ltd
Newton Road
Manor Royal
Crawley
West Sussex RH10 9TT
Tel: +44 (0)1293 423700
Fax: +44 (0)1293 403080

Steam cleaners and dental supplies

Zahn Laboratory
Medcare House
Centurion Close
Gillingham Business Park
Gillingham
Kent ME8 0SB
Tel: +44 (0)8700 102047
Fax: +44 (0)8700 102087
www.henryschein.co.uk
email: zahnlab@henryschein.co.uk

Conservation associations, advice and further study in the UK and worldwide

There are a number of advisory bodies and professional organisations in the field of conservation where information can be obtained on training and other matters relating to the conservation of ceramics.

United Kingdom Institute for Conservation of Historic & Artistic Works (UKIC)
6 Whitehorse Mews
Westminster Bridge Road
London SE1 7QD
UK
(Publishers of *Conservation News* and head-quarters of the Ceramic and Glass Conservation Group, which meets twice yearly)

Scottish Society for Conservation & Restoration (SSCR)
Department of Archaeology

University of Glasgow
10 The Square
Glasgow G12 8QQ
UK

Conservation Bureau, Historic Scotland
Stenhouse Conservation Centre &
Conservation Bureau
3 Stenhouse Mill Lane
Edinburgh EH11 3LR
UK

International Institute For Conservation
6 Buckingham Street
London WC2 6BA
UK

The Conservation Unit, Museums & Galleries
Commission
16 Queen Anne's Gate
London SW1 9AA
UK

International Council Of Museums (ICOM)
Maison de l'Unesco
1 Rue Miollis
Paris Cedex 15
France

International Centre for the Study &
Preservation and Restoration of Cultural
Material (ICCROM)
13 Via di S. Michele
Rome 1-00153
Italy

American Institute for Conservation (AIC)
3545 Willamsbugh Lane
Washington DC 20008
USA

Canadian Conservation Institute
1030 Innes Road
Ottawa K1A 0M8
Canada

Getty Conservation Institute
4503 Glencoe Avenue
Marina del Rey
California 90292–6537
USA

Institute for the Conservation of Cultural
Material (ICCM)

PO Box 1638, Canberra ACT
Australia

Manufacturers and suppliers, USA

Many of the materials recommended in this
book can be purchased from general hardware
stores or good graphic supply stores. There are
also a number of general craft suppliers which
stock a range of conservation materials, as well
as specialist suppliers of specific products. Only
suppliers of products available in the USA have
been listed here. If you require a product that is
not available in the USA, consult a specialist
supplier for a US equivalent or order from a
foreign supplier (see UK list).

Adhesives

Acryloid B-72
Fisher Scientific

Rhoplex AC–33 and Araldite
CIBA-Geigy Co.
Formulated Systems Group
4917 Dawn Avenue
East Lansing, MI 48823
Tel: + 517 351 5900
Fax: + 517 351 9003

Devcon adhesives
The above suppliers or

Devcon Corp.
30 Endicott Street
Danvers, MA 01923
Tel: + 978 777 1100
Fax: + 978 774 0516

White neutral ph adhesives and superglue
Hardware stores or lumber yards

Acetone and hydrogen peroxide
Hardware stores or pharmacists

Brushes and airbrushes
Graphic supply shops

Cleaning products

Proprietary detergents and water softeners
Supermarkets and hardware stores

Zynolyte paint remover, poultice materials, and general chemical cleaners
Hardware stores or Conservation Resources International, Fisher Scientific

Devcon Magicbond
Devcon Corp.

Finishing materials

Micro-mesh abrading system
Micro-Surface Finishing
PO Box 70
1217 West 3rd street
Wilton IA 52778
Tel: + 563 732 3240
Fax: + 563 732 3390
www.micro-surface.com
email: sales@netins.net

Renaissance wax
Cutlery Specialities
22 Morris Lane
Great Neck, NY 11024
Tel: + 516 829 5899
Fax: + 516 773 8076
www.restorationproduct.com
email: Dennis13@aol.com

Tri-m-ite sandpaper/magic tape
3M
3M Twin Center
St. Paul
Minnesota 55144-100
Tel: + 651 733 1110
Fax: + 651 733 9973

General conservation and art specialists

Conservation Resources International
800–H Forbes Place
Springfield, VA 22151
Tel: + 703 3217730
Fax: + 703 321 0629

Fisher Scientific
600 Business Centre Drive
Pittsburgh, PA 15205/1334
Tel: + 412 490 8505
Fax: + 412 490 8700

General craft supplies, calcium sulphate (plaster of Paris) and other plaster
Conservation Resources International, Fisher Scientific

Milliput
Micro-mark
340 Snyder Avenue
Berkley Heights
NJ 07922
Tel: + 908 464 2984
Fax: + 908 665 9383
www.micromark.com

The VLS Corporation
(Legacy Distributing)
1011 Industrial Court
Moscow Mills, MO 63362
Tel: + 636 356 4888
Fax: + 636 356 4877

Pigments and general art supplies

Powder pigments, Golden products
Graphic supply shops or Conservation Resources International

Specialist conservation equipment
General Conservation Resources International, Fisher Scientific

Small scales and instruments
Rubin & Son, USA Inc.
96 Spring Street
New York, NY 10012
Tel: + 212 966 6300
Fax: + 212 966 6354

Client-Conservator agreement

It is recommended that the conservator should enter into a simple form of agreement with the client on delivery of the broken object for repair, covering such items as the work to be carried out, the price, payment, insurance and non-collection of the object etc. An example of such an agreement which may be used is set out overleaf. However, the precise terms to be used are a matter of individual choice or negotiation with the client and the conservator may wish to adopt modified terms from those recommended. This example applies to English law.

No responsibility whatsoever is accepted by the authors or publishers of this book for this agreement and, in particular, as to whether it achieves its intended purposes. The conservator is advised to take his/her own legal advice before using these terms or any variations to them. It should particularly be noted that the courts have power to disallow certain types of terms in certain contracts deemed to be 'unfair' and it is possible that some of the terms set out on the following page could be challenged on these grounds.

Terms and conditions

A This agreement is made between the Conservator and the Client whose respective details appear in the particulars overleaf ('the Particulars').

B The work The Conservator will carry out the conservation/restoration work specified in the Particulars ('the work') to the object or objects therein specified ('the object'). Whilst the Conservator will endeavour to carry out the work with reasonable care and skill no responsibility to the Client is undertaken to that effect and the Conservator shall in no circumstances be liable to the Client for any damage to or loss or destruction of the object whether or not caused by the negligence of the Conservator or any other person and however caused.

C The price Where an estimate is given by the Conservator such estimate is open for acceptance by the Client for a period of two months failing which it may at the sole discretion of the Conservator be revised. The Conservator will endeavour to ensure that the final price chargeable to the Client is within the estimate (plus any agreed additional costs) but reserves the right to increase the price above the estimate where the work required proves to be greater and/or more time-consuming than originally anticipated.

D Payment Unless the contrary appears in the Particulars then payment of the final price notified to the Client by the Conservator is due from the Client upon collection of the conserved/restored object.

E Insurance The object remains at the entire risk of the Client. It is accordingly the Client's responsibility to insure the object in such sums and for such risks as the Client shall think fit and no such insurance shall be taken out by the Conservator.

F Cancellation Where the Conservator has commenced the work and this Agreement is cancelled by the Client prior to completion the Conservator shall in lieu of damages for breach of contract be entitled to require the payment of that part of the estimated price proportionate to the amount of the work carried out.

G Duration The Conservator will endeavour to complete the work with all due diligence but any dates given or periods of time quoted are estimates only and shall not be the ground for any claim for loss or compensation against the Conservator.

H Completion Unless the contrary appears in the Particulars the Conservator shall notify the Client of completion of the work by post or telephone to the address or telephone number for the Client noted in the Particulars. It is the Client's responsibility to notify any change of address or telephone number.

I Collection It shall be the obligation of the Client to collect the object after notification by the Conservator of the completion of the work. If the object is not collected within six months of the date of such notification then title to the object shall pass to the Conservator who shall be free to sell the same and from the net proceeds to recover such sums as may be due to the Conservator under this Agreement. The Conservator shall then hold the balance of such proceeds (if any) for the Client for a further period of twelve months after such sale but shall thereafter be entitled to retain the same for the Conservator's own benefit if not claimed by the Client by the end of that period.

J Copyright The Conservator retains the copyright in all reports drawings or photographs prepared under this

Agreement which may not be reproduced in whole or in part without the Conservator's consent which may be given on terms or declined with or without reason.

K This Agreement is governed by the provisions of English law.

Name, address and telephone number of Conservator

Date

Name, address and telephone number of Client

Description of object

Agreed conservation/restoration work
The Conservator will notify of completion by telephone

Estimated cost   £ + VAT

Additional costs Materials, carriage,
research, visits, photographs etc   £ + VAT

Agreement
The Conservator agrees to repair the Object and the Client delivers it for repair subject to the Terms and Conditions set out overleaf.

Signature of Client   **Date**

Signature of Conservator   **Date**

Suggested further reading

Atterbury, Paul & Maureen Batkin *The Dictionary of Minton* (Antique Collectors' Club 1990)

Benner, Larsen, *Moulding & Casting of Museum Objects* (Vester Kopi, Denmark 1994)

Black, Dr. J., *English Polychrome Delftware and its Repair* (UKIC conservation paper 1993)

Buys, Susan & Victoria Oakley, *The Conservation and Restoration of Ceramics* (Butterworth-Heinemann 1993)

Charles, Bernard H., *Pottery & Porcelain* (David & Charles 1974)

Cohen, David Harris & Catherine Hess, *Looking at European Ceramics – A Guide to Technical Terms* (Getty/BMP 1993)

Du Boulay, Anthony, *Chinese Porcelain* (Weidenfeld & Nicolson 1963)

Duckett, Graham, *Creative Airbrushing* (The Promotional Reprint Company Ltd for Bookmart Ltd 1992)

Godden, Geoffrey, *An Illustrated Encyclopedia of British Pottery & Porcelain* (Magna Books 1992)

Godden, Geoffrey, *Coalport & Coalbrookdale Porcelain* (Herbert Jenkins 1970)

Green, Lorna R., *Cleaning Agents – Considerations for Ceramic Conservators* British Museum (UKIC conservation paper 1992)

Halfpenny, Pat, *English Earthenware Figures* (Antique Collectors Club 1991)

Health & Safety Executive, *A step by step guide to COSHH assessment*

Horrie, C.V., *Materials for Conservation* (Butterworth-Heinemann 1996)

Kingery, W. David & Pamela B Vandiver, *Ceramic Masterpieces* (Free Press 1986)

Money, John, *Lighting Requirements for Conservators & Restorers* (Paper to accompany CLE Design Ltd catalogue 1993)

Pearce, Emma, *The Materials and Techniques of Painting* (Jonathan Stephenson Thames & Hudson 1989)

Pearce, Emma, *Pigments & Brushes* (UKIC Publication 1993)

Reynolds, Dinah, *Worcester Porcelain* (Ashmolean/Christies Handbooks 1989)

Robson, Maureen A., *Methods of restoration and conservation of Bronze Age pottery urns at the British Museum, early advances in conservation* (ed. V Daniels) (British Museum occasional paper no. 65. 1988

Rodwell, Jenny, *Painting with Acrylics* (Macdonald 1986)

Savage, G. & H. Newman, *An Illustrated Dictionary of Ceramics* (Thames & Hudson

Science for Conservators Various authors (The conservation unit of the Museums & Galleries Commission and Routledge 1992)
Volume 1 – An Introduction to Materials
Volume 2 – Cleaning
Volume 3 – Adhesives & Coatings
UKIC–CGCG Conference Post Prints Various authors
 Adhesives & Consolidants for Ceramics and Related Materials 1997
 Back to Basics 1996
 Dust, Dirt & Debris 1997
 Gilding, Lustre & Metals 1994
 Modelling Moulding & Casting 1998
 Problems and Solutions 1999
 Shared Experiences 1996
 Study Trip – Amsterdam 1998

Van Lemmen, Hans, *The Preservation of Delftware Tiles in British Architecture* (English Heritage conservation paper 1994)

Index